MW01224240

AMERICA
SAFE AGAIN

★ ★ ★ ★ ★ ★ ★ ★ ★ ★

10 PRAYERS
TO TURN THE TIDE

Don Black
with Jack Watts

Published by CTVN Media
1 Signal Hill Drive
Wall, PA 15148
E-mail: ctvnmedia@ctvn.org

Cover & Interior by Randy Drake Designs & Riverstone Group, LLC

Special Sales:
Pastors, church and small group leaders may receive special discounts when
purchasing this book in quantities. For more information please e-mail requests to
ctvnmedia@ctvn.org.

ISBN: 978-0-9859384-8-2

Printed in USA

DEDICATION

I want to thank all who helped in making this book possible:

- To Bill Federer for his tremendous knowledge of history and red-hot passion for God and America.

- Special thanks to Randy Drake and Ernest Pullen for their gifted art design.

- To Crystal Bynum and Amanda Gaines-Borders for keen eyes in editing and research.

- To my loving and patient family who have suffered for the cause of this important message.

- An extra special thank-you to my wonderful wife, Teri, who makes everything better.

I dedicate this book to my mom, Harriet Kelsey Black, whose ancestor William Kelsey came to this land in 1632, in search of freedom to worship, and to my children and future generations, whom I pray will fight to preserve and protect the spiritual foundation of our great nation.

Most importantly, I commit this book to our Heavenly Father and to the Bride of Christ; Whom He is building up so that the gates of Hell will not prevail. May His Kingdom Quickly Come!

PREFACE

Critical Times

I n the winter of 2015, I released the book *America Needs A Miracle.* It made it clear that no matter what candidates were nominated and ultimately who would win the national election in fall of the next year, they would not be able to solve our problems. What our nation desperately needed was a miracle from God! We have drifted too far and too fast from our biblical foundation for any political party or elected official who could "fix" America.

In January of 2016, we had a guest on Cornerstone Television's flagship program, *Real Life,* whose visit shocked me. He reported that in the Presidential Election of 2012 more than 25 million Christians, who were registered to vote, didn't even turn out at the polls. How could that be?

Knowing how important the 2016 Presidential Election was to America's future, we felt led by the Holy Spirit to challenge Christians citizens to first pray, fast, and then to go out and vote the way God led. Having made the determination that the Lord was leading us forward, *In God We Trust* was born. God supernaturally helped us produce a TV special and a website that featured national Christian leaders. They called for

Christian patriots to sign the *In God We Trust* proclamation and make a pledge to vote.

The response to this campaign was overwhelming! It far exceeded our expectations. This confirmed that in America the majority believe that our country needs to turn back to our biblically based foundation. Based on much prayer, we made the determination to continue to bring these Christians together and see real change in Washington, DC. It is our purpose to move forward and have a positive impact on our beloved nation—just as our forefathers had done.

Today, we face enemies from within and without. Our struggle is not only in the natural world but, more importantly, in the spiritual world. This is why Christians, believers like you and me, need to take a stand for all that is right, while also repudiating the lies and combating the darkness that attempts to dominate every level of our culture.

To this cause we dedicate *Make America Safe Again*. To turn the tide on terror, we need to be involved. I am committed to using my time, my talents, and my strength to make America great and safe again. In this campaign, I have asked Jack Watts, a friend for many years, to help me.

It is our prayer that *Make America Safe Again* will be a blessing to you, but we pray that it will stir your heart. So, before we begin, please join me in the following prayer.

Don Black

Prayer for
In God We Trust Initiative

Please Join Us in the Following Prayer.

Our Gracious God and Loving Heavenly Father:
From the very beginning of America's foundation,
From the time the Pilgrims landed at Plymouth Rock,
And the Puritans established Massachusetts Bay Colony,
You put into their hearts the idea that America was destined
To become a mighty nation—a diverse and unique people.
The original settlers believed they were creating a
City on a Hill—
A unique nation for the entire world to behold and emulate.
This was their purpose and
The corporate dream of our founders.

For all of those who sailed from Europe to the New Land,
Enduring hardship in the wilderness and extreme deprivation,
They founded a new nation,
Forged out of beautiful but barren land.
They did so joyfully, with a willing heart,
Because of their love for You.
They counted it all joy to suffer adversity and deprivation,
Simply to be able to worship You as they saw fit,
Without restraint.
This goal was so important that

They risked their lives to achieve it.
Indeed, our forefathers were mighty men and women of God.
Based on their original intent and
What burned deep within their hearts,
Praiseworthy values emerged that
Drove them relentlessly forward.
Over time, their foundational beliefs became
Our Puritan Work Ethic.

For more than two centuries
This was the bedrock upon which we thrived
But many no longer hold these values in high esteem.
Instead, we now live in an era where godless Progressivism
Dominates our schools, universities,
Entertainment, and the media.
Rather than acknowledge You and give thanks,
Like our forefathers,

This generation arrogantly mocks Your name,
Your Word, and Your Son,
While proudly denouncing the great cloud of witnesses
That went before them.
These arrogant men and women repudiate the contributions
Of all the past generations that made America
A beacon of light.
Now, we face a crisis, as the perils of Islamic Terrorism threaten
Our very existence—but the self-important Progressives,
Who continue to dominate many areas of our government,

Refuse to acknowledge that our only hope is to return to You.

As Your redeemed children, the faithful remnant who continue
To make a conscious choice to honor You and to seek Your will,
We humbly bow our knees before You today, and ask
For Your forgiveness for all that we have done as a nation
To act willfully and to behave disrespectfully toward You.
Having drifted so far from our foundational roots and values,
We are without excuse. Nevertheless, we do ask for Your mercy.
Help us return to our faith and to the eternal values
That once made us strong.
Let us once again be a City on a Hill
For the entire world to follow. We ask this humbly, in the name
Of Jesus Christ, our Lord, our Redeemer, and our Savior,

Amen.

CONTENTS

Introduction. 13

1. We Must Make a Stand 25

2. Perverting the Truth—the Enemy Within 33

3. Standing Firm Against a False God. 51

4. The Historical Tradition of Christianity in America . 73

5. Our Forefathers Sought God's Will 83

6. The Power of Prayer, Fasting, and Repentance 103

Conclusion. 117

Appendix 121

INTRODUCTION

*You are the light of the world. A city set on a hill cannot be
hidden. Nor do men light a lamp, and put it under the
peck-measure, but on the lampstand; and it gives light to
all who are in the house. Let your light shine before
men in such a way that they may see your good works,
and glorify your Father who is in heaven*
(Matthew 5:14-16, NAS).

When asked, nearly every Christian will readily acknowledge that God has a purpose for his or her life. This belief is a quintessential part of being a Christian. It is such a deeply held value that it is common for people like us to regularly reevaluate our purpose in life. By understanding that our life is found in Christ, and that our real purpose is found in serving Him, it provides an operating guide and overarching framework for life. This is the way it is for nearly all of us. Because you are reading a book like this one, we are confident that you too share this worldview.

When we get out of step with God or His purpose, which happens to all of us from time to time, we begin to experience the adverse consequences of our actions. Sometimes, our penalty for walking outside of the will of God can be quite severe. So much so that the end result drives us back to our Heavenly

Father in repentance. Like disobedient children, we return to Him in humility, most likely broken and hurting.

The longer we are believers, if we are focusing on God's will, the more firmly His precepts take hold of our lives. Through Holy Spirit pruning, the way we live becomes more Christ-like, and the fruits of the Spirit become more visibly apparent. Through this spiritual life journey, we gradually grow into the mature men and women God intended for us to be when He called us to Himself years earlier. This is the process of discipleship and the way the Body of Christ works.

As part of being a mature man or woman in Christ, we become salt and light to our fallen world. This is true for us, not just individually, but also collectively. Recognizing and understanding our collective role as believers, which is to stand for Christ in the midst of a depraved culture, is precisely what *Make America Safe Again* is all about.

Many of us understand the role God plays in our lives as individuals. We comprehend this part of our personal Christian walk quite well. In fact, it's our daily focus nearly all the time. Independently, we know how we are supposed to function in the Body of Christ.

At the same time, many of us are not nearly as certain about what is expected of us as Christian citizens in the United States of America. There is quite a bit of confusion about this. In fact, there are many perspectives, running the gambit from having nothing to do with the "worldliness" of politics to the other end of the spectrum, which is the belief that we should dominate our nation. That is to essentially exercise "Dominion" over it.

So, what is our role supposed to be? What does God expect of us, and how can we be as faithful corporately as we are learning to be individually? These are some of the questions we intend to address in *Make America Safe Again: 10 Prayers to Turn The Tide*, using the example of our forefathers as our guide.

To understand the role we need to play, there are some steps we need to take. First, let's take a good look at exactly where we are as a nation. Being rigorously honest, we must ask ourselves some hard questions.

- What is the Christian's responsibility as a citizen?

- Are we Christians fulfilling the purpose God has set before us, or aren't we? If we are not, then what do we need to do?

- Do we actually understand what is happening in America, or do we not?

- Are we missing anything? If so, what is it? And, more importantly, what can we do about it?

Our history is a grand one, but it is not without blemish. Only by understanding who we once were can we know who we are now. More importantly, this will also tell us who we are supposed to be.

Once we understand this, in our role as American citizens, we can learn to be the empowered men and women Christ intended us to be. As the British Parliamentarian Edmund Burke poignantly said in the nineteenth century, "The only thing necessary for Evil to triumph is for good men to do nothing."

As Christians, we are called to be good men and women, precisely as Edmund Burke described. This is not only true of us individually but also of us corporately.

Why should it be any other way?

As believers and important members of the Body of Christ, we have a role to play in correcting the direction our beloved nation is heading. We simply cannot stand idly by and allow Evil to triumph. That's a given, but to be effective, we must understand the exact nature of the Evil that confronts our freedoms. The more we know about what this Evil is, the more effectively we answer Jesus' call to be light and salt to America.

We have enemies from without and enemies from within—both are doing everything they can to weaken and eventually destroy our nation's biblical foundation. To make matters worse, they have been more effective at quietly promoting and establishing darkness in our nation than most realize. This is why we are challenging Christian citizens to take a stand for Almighty God and for our country—right here and right now. It's what we must do. We have no other choice—not and be the good men and women Burke described.

Beginning right now, this very minute, using today as our starting point, our goal is to help men and women of faith. We want to help people like you to unite through prayer, fasting and repentance—to lift up families, cities, states, and our beloved nation to Almighty God.

Prayer is powerful, and it is an effective counterforce to the evils that beset us at home and abroad.

Through our active involvement, by beseeching Almighty God corporately as well as individually, and being fully united in purpose, we intend to watch God transform this great nation. Our goal is to bring America back into alignment with our traditional Judeo-Christian value system. This, and only this, is what will make America truly great and safe again. If we choose instead to do nothing, then Evil will surely triumph, and the nation we love so dearly will fail to fulfill God's purpose.

Our battle is for the hearts and minds of millions of badly deceived Americans. We are not alone in our struggle. Our work is that of the Lord, and we are confident that "Greater is He who" is in us than "he who is in the world," 1 John 4:4.

We have no question about this. Nor do we have doubts about our purpose, none whatsoever. We are crystal clear about our heart's desires and about our goal.

Bolstered by this assurance, and the conviction that our Heavenly Father is with and before us, we intend to confront Evil—the false god of Radical Islamic Terrorists and the equally false belief system of American Progressives—with the truth. One is an external threat, although they have employed domestic terrorism as one of their tools for waging war.

A Fight from Within

Our other enemy is attacking America from within. The Progressives' plan is to change our society by imposing their anti-American and anti-God worldview on our impressionable young people. Tragically, the Progressives have already poisoned an entire generation of our kids and grandkids with their heretical perspective.

Regardless of how far we have drifted away from God, as the unified Body of Christ, we intend to turn the tragedy of our current state of affairs into victory. This is a giant goal, but all things are possible through Christ (Philippians 4:13). United in Him, we can see a giant change. The days of Christians sitting idly by and allowing Evil to triumph in America are over, and they will never return—unless we allow it.

But who are we? And how is it that can we make such bold statements? We are Christian citizens united! *In God We Trust,* is a ministry outreach dedicated to God's truth. It is our prayer to awaken, arouse, and empower Christians in the United States by the millions.

Our message is this: **America has a special and unique purpose—one inspired by God and birthed by our founding fathers centuries ago. Based on their Christian convictions, they created America to be a "city on a hill." Their vision was for us to be a beacon of freedom for the entire world to see and emulate.** This purpose never changed, but the direction of the United States certainly has, especially in the past half century. By a wide margin, we have wandered away from the Truth and fallen away in the opposite direction.

America used to espouse Freedom of Religion. Now, we promote Freedom from Restraint, championing godlessness and perversion. We are rapidly becoming a nation where everybody is free to do whatever is right in his or her own eyes.

Progressives, who relentlessly dominate our culture through the media and the educational system, rigidly enforces "Totalitarianism of Thought," refusing to allow any deviation from an approved narrative. To have a biblical worldview, is archaic, ignorant, and unscientific.

The contempt for us is so severe that expressing our Christian perspective is close to being considered "hate speech." Despite losing elections, political correctness remains dominant in our land. Tragically, this has made millions of Christians timid and fearful to speak the Truth. Rather than stand our ground against this dominant juggernaut, believers have demurred, choosing to remain silent. We have been retreating for decades, but this has to change.

The time to reverse this trend is now. We must reclaim our nation and return it to its original intent. It is time to reinstate our traditional values. If we do not do it now, our opportunity may be lost forever.

It is our objective at *In God We Trust,* to facilitate a transformation in America. We intend to do this by calling Christians to account. Believing that the Word of God is accurate and true, we invoke His promise, that if "My people, who are called by My name, humble themselves and pray, and seek my face and turn from their wicked ways, then I will hear from heaven, will forgive their sin, and will heal their land" (2 Chronicles 7:14, NAS).

We believe this is true—literally true. This is a biblical promise. It is not a high-minded but meaningless statement. What Almighty God says is trustworthy and true.

This Scripture provides us with our marching orders, which we intend to follow. Therefore, at *In God We Trust,* we are launching an ongoing effort to call Christians to pray, fast, and become active in making our nation accountable. We intend to confront the godlessness of our culture head-on, calling the church and America to repent of our national sins.

Our goal is to reestablish the traditional foundational beliefs of our forefathers, as provided in the US Constitution. This is not just a sweet sentiment. It is our intention to make this a reality. It can be done. Our children and grandchildren's freedoms depend on it.

We have a plan to launch an annual initiative with four strategic events—each tied to major patriotic and cultural days in our national calendar. Beginning with 9/11, which focuses on keeping our nation safe, we will have three additional programs—one for Thanksgiving week, Martin Luther King, Jr. Day, and Memorial Day.

To be everything we can be for Christ, we need to have a clear understanding of where we are as a nation. This starts by recognizing our enemy from within, Progressivism, and coming to terms with it.

Before addressing Progressivism, here is an introductory prayer. Pray it with us as often as you desire:

Our Ways Are No Longer Your Ways

Please Join Us in the Following Prayer

Father in Heaven,
We have wandered so far from You,
From Your ways, from Your leading,
From Your desires, and from Your purpose.
At first, it didn't seem like this was such a great distance,
But now that we look back, it has become clear
That our stubborn willfulness has led us
To a barren spiritual wilderness, where millions,
Repudiating Your Word,
Call right wrong and wrong right.

As a nation, in our arrogance and self-righteousness,
We still speak Your name, but it is without reverence.
We still want Your blessing,
And confidently believe we have
A right to ask for it,
But we do not look to You for Leadership,
Nor do we consider obeying Your will to be important.

We acknowledge this is the true report,
And confess our complicity
In being docile, apathetic, and complicit,
As the forces of Darkness
Have usurped our traditions, our heritage,
And our purpose,
Redefining history to justify their godless perspective.
Let us remember that it is always
Our duty to seek the Truth.

We stand in the shadow of generations of
Christian patriots,
Those who fought the good fight
So that we would remain free
To worship You in peace and prosperity,
Free from impediment.
But now we face new obstacles.
A new spirit has emerged,
One whose haughtiness and pride
Makes it sneer in disdain,
As they mock Your name and Your people,
Calling us ignorant,
Uninformed, and dangerous to

Their secular globalism.
As believers in You and
Your willingness to restore America,
We ask that You hear our prayers,
As we bow before You,
Repenting of our societal sins and
Beseeching You to heal our land.
We ask this, not because we are deserving,
But because of Your love, mercy, and grace.

Amen.

CHAPTER 1

We Must Make a Stand

*The things which you have heard from me in the presence of
many witnesses, entrust these to faithful men who will be able to
teach others also* (II Timothy 2:2, NAS).

I t's easy to say, "The only thing necessary for Evil to triumph
is for good men to do nothing." This is certainly a very noble,
uplifting sentiment, but what does it mean? What is the
nature of the Evil we must confront—both domestically and
internationally? And, given our current situation in the United
States, in the late teens of the twenty-first century, how do we
effectively counteract each of these Evils—Progressivism and
Radical Islamic Terrorism?

First, for our prayers and actions to reflect God's leading
accurately where the Progressive worldview is concerned, we
must clearly differentiate between our Christian perspective and
the belief system of our Progressive adversaries. By clarifying the
differences, we will be better able to address what needs to be
done to nullify their adverse impact upon our youth. This is our
primary domestic problem.

Second, we must also understand and completely accept the

anti-American goals of Radical Islam. Plain and simple, they want to destroy and subjugate the United States of America. For them, there is no middle ground. From their perspective, conquest and subjection to Allah is what America's future will be. To be true to Allah, there can be no other result. If we refuse to become Muslim, we must die—period.

For us to be effective in thwarting this Evil anti-American goal, we must come to understand why Islamic beliefs can never be peacefully integrated into our way of life. By nature, this worldview gravitates to extremism. Obviously not all Muslims are terrorists, but the percentage who are is alarmingly high. Thus, it is a serious mistake to believe that peaceful integration of Islam into our society can ever become a reality. To believe that it can is as foolhardy as believing you can domesticate a cobra.

We also need to assert that stating the objectives of Islam is not being Islamaphobic. Despite what the Progressives say to the contrary, this isn't hate speech. It's just being straightforward with the truth, which is something that has become offensive to Leftists in our politically correct society.

It is only in recent years, when Progressive thinking began to supersede and replace our traditional Judeo-Christian worldview, that fear of being straightforward with the truth became a problem. Having traveled the wrong road for so long, to simply state the truth is now considered "hate speech" by a growing portion of our society. Nevertheless, at *In God We Trust*, this is exactly what we intend to do, not only in this book but also in everything we do.

"If you would do the best with your life, find out what God is doing in your generation and throw yourself wholly into it." - Arthur Wallis

Our purpose is to seek God's will for our generation, and when we discern it, to follow it to the letter. Our aim is not new to American history. We have a rich tradition. Seeking God's will—which includes corporate prayer to Almighty God for wisdom, guidance, and leadership—has a robust place, beginning with the Pilgrims and the Puritans.

Our mission is not against the law or a violation of the separation of church and state. Our intention is neither new nor novel, but it is biblical and Constitutional. The long and treasured part of our history will be explained, using primary documents from the historical record. While this is not a history book, it most definitely is historically accurate.

Finally, we intend to be crystal clear and very specific about what each of us can do to help change America. This includes linking arms with us at *In God We Trust*. Each of us has a personal mandate from Heaven to be faithful to His calling, but we also have corporate responsibilities as citizens. At *In God We Trust*, we intend to be faithful to these duties.

In our personal lives, it is our responsibility to be faithful to the Holy Spirit's leading. Collectively, as members of the Body of

Christ, we have a corporate role to play as well. We know this—sort of—but the conviction that it produces in us is not nearly as powerful as it is for us individually.

One of the things we want to do is help you understand what our corporate role is for America. By the time you have finished *Make America Safe Again*, it is our belief that you will have a much clearer understanding of what is happening in the world, both domestically and internationally.

The value of being a part of a national effort of unified believers will also become much more apparent to you. By being enlightened about the Evils that threaten our American way of life, and our very existence as a nation, you will also be better equipped to address our Heavenly Father about our adversaries in your personal prayer life. This is obviously important, but our main focus here concerns our national wellbeing.

As our united voices are raised to God, our ability to watch Him restore our nation will increase proportionately. What we are pursuing at *In God We Trust* is a high calling, and our dedication and faithfulness are critical. There is no downside to praying and fasting for the safety of the United States of America—none whatsoever.

With this in mind, here is a prayer for you to use as you wish.

At the end of each chapter, we have added a prayer.

We Are Not Where God Wants Us to Be

Please Join Us in the Following Prayer

Heavenly Father,
As Your children,
We come before You today to confess our national sins.
Our hearts are heavy because of
The enormity of our transgressions.
We have discarded our spiritual foundation
And rejected your values.
We have ridiculed the truth of Your Word,
Championing Progressivism instead.
We have embraced numerous false gods
In the name of religious tolerance.
We have endorsed perversion,
Accepting deviant lifestyles as normal.
We have exploited the hardworking
To reward the corrupt lavishly.
We have excused laziness and
Rewarded non-workers with never-ending welfare.

We have killed our unborn
And defended abortion as an honorable choice.
We have failed to discipline our children,
Creating an arrogant, indulgent generation.

We have accepted those who abuse power,
Never holding them to account.
We have ignored the corrupt use of public funds,
Never blinking an eye.

We have allowed the institutionalization of
Bribery to become standard business.
We have scoffed at the values of our forefathers
And called ourselves enlightened.
We consume so much alcohol and drugs that
Millions of us stay high daily.
We have polluted our minds with pornography,
Calling our addiction enlightenment.

Father, these are just a small fraction
Of our societal sins, which we recognize.
We have called right wrong, while legalizing wrong
And defending it as being right.
We have drifted so far from your precepts that millions
Of Americans no longer have an accurate moral compass
That points them to honorable, righteous endeavors.
We know who we are, who we have become,
And the price we have to pay;
But we also know and understand
The depth of Your love for us,
And the magnitude of your mercy and grace
Toward the American people.
This is why we come to You today,

In humility, on bended knee,
Fasting and repenting, as we beseech You
To spare us from calamity.
Even though we are undeserving,
Father, keep the United States of America,

The nation we have loved our entire lives, safe from terror.
We ask this in the name of Jesus Christ,
Your Son and our Savior,
Amen.

CHAPTER 2

Perverting the Truth–
the Enemy Within

*For even though they knew God, they did not honor Him as God,
or give thanks; but they became futile in their speculations, and
their foolish heart was darkened. Professing to be wise, they became
fools, and exchanged the glory of the incorruptible God for an im-
age in the form of corruptible man* (Romans 1:21-23a, NAS).

Most of you are Christians who maintain a Conservative
perspective. If this is correct, you take the Constitution
seriously. You understand that it is the foundation upon
which our democracy stands. You also know that the Rule
of law is fundamental to who we are. Nobody is above the law
or, at least, nobody is supposed to be above it. For us, these are
deeply held convictions, but we maintain numerous others as
well.

We know that our rights are inalienable. Like you, all of us at
In God We Trust believe this is true. Plus, we believe these rights
have been bestowed upon us by Almighty God. This means the
government cannot take them away from us, nor can anyone
infringe upon them. They are by divine right—period.

Being inalienable, this ensures that they cannot be revoked or nullified—not under any circumstances. They are our birthright as citizens of the United States. More than any other aspect of our identity as Americans, this is what has historically differentiated us from other nations, and it has made us the envy of the entire world.

We have numerous inalienable rights. Our ability to worship as we choose is one of them. So is our right to assemble and our ability to speak freely. These rights are intrinsic to who we are as Americans. We cherish them. They are as venerated by us as some of our sacred beliefs. They are the essence of what makes us American and the specific reason why we are a special and unique nation.

As Conservative Christians, these rights, along with numerous others, constitute the core of our identity as citizens. When we hear about American Exceptionalism, our inalienable rights are the foundation for the greatness of the United States. Without these rights, we would not be exceptional in any way other than in wealth and military power. This is how important these rights are to us, and this will never change. For nearly all of us, we couldn't stop believing these core values are true, or ever imagine our nation existing without them.

On the other hand, the Progressives scoff at the concept of "self-evident truths." To them, our founder's conviction about inalienable rights is a failed experiment of the past. It's some fanciful notion that has no place in the modern world.

Progressives, on the other hand, see themselves as enlightened men and women, and they know better. To them, twenty-first-century America has evolved far beyond such "foolishness" or, at least, it has for most intelligent Americans. Those who continue to believe in fanciful nonsense like inalienable rights are people "who cling to their guns and their Bibles." Ignorant by nature, these uninformed fools are living in the past. The future does not belong to them. It belongs to the enlightened Progressives.

According to them, to believe in inalienable rights, because God is the One who "bestowed" all of these rights on Americans, you have to believe in Him. Not only would you have to believe that God is real, but you would also have to believe that He is active in the affairs of our nation, which they do not believe He is. Such mystical notions are little more than superstitious drivel, according to the enlightened.

To Christians, God's active involvement in our lives makes perfect sense, but Progressives consider our mindset to be dangerous to our democracy. To them, our Christian worldview is the enemy of progress and fundamental fairness.

Progressives think they deal with facts, not irrational mythology. Because of this, they think they are the only ones who possess the truth. We do not. Because they see the world as it is, through their Progressive lens, they are "wise". Our lens, by way of contrast, is essentially flawed, making us fools. Since this is obviously true, it is acceptable for Progressives to scoff at our Conservative Christian perspective. It's sport for them.

After all, we are nothing more than unenlightened misfits. We deserve the mocking we receive.

To them, what we believe is unacceptable. We are homophobic, Islamophobic, woman haters, racists, all of which are contemptible viewpoints. Although they cannot stop us from believing in God, they think they can stop us from having any significant impact on society. This is precisely what they have been trying to do in earnest for several decades.

To them, it is our faith in God, and our belief in American exceptionalism, that is holding back our society. If they can effectively squelch us, which they intend to do, regardless of what is required to accomplish this task, they think they are making progress, and America is moving in the right direction.

Thus, being devious and deceitful in dealing with us, is not wrong—not if the end is to further the Progressive cause. Winning is their goal, their only goal, so whatever it takes to accomplish this task is moral and right. For a Progressive, the ends always justify the means.

From our perspective, we are horrified by what the Progressives think and what they sometimes do. We are constantly shocked and appalled by their seemingly unethical behavior. This is because we do not really understand them or what they believe.

Their behavior has been so outrageous to us that we dismiss what they do as being crazy. We have not considered it worth the time it would take to understand them. This has been a serious error on our part.

For instance, at the Democratic National Convention in 2012, when the entire delegation booed God, while we watched on TV, we were appalled, angered, and horrified. Collectively, our mouth's dropped in shock and astonishment that any American would do such a dishonorable and disrespectful thing. Although our response is understandable, it also revealed our lack of understanding about what Progressivism really is. This has to change.

Just as we cannot defeat Radical Islamic Terrorism without naming it and understanding what it is, we cannot confront and defeat Progressive ideology without recognizing it and understanding its underlying belief system.

At its core is spiritual conflict with Christianity. To them, it is our God, the God of Christianity, that is the problem in America. He is not the solution. That we believe in God, along with American Exceptionalism, is what has caused most of the problems in the world today. This is why the Progressives are hostile toward Christianity, but have no apparent animosity toward any other religions, including Islam.

For them, America has become strong and rich, not because of God's blessing, but because we have robbed and subjugated other people and other nations, all in the name of God. There is nothing special about us other than the fact that we have become very skilled at using the wealth of the world for our own benefit. Shamefully, all of our achievements have been at the expense of others, who are less fortunate.

This is why Progressives are constantly apologizing for America and believe it is our responsibility to make reparations for every real or perceived injustice in the world today. Because they believe it is our distorted belief in God that is at the root of all of America's crimes, it's perfectly logical for them to boo God at the Democratic National Convention. In the minds of those who participated, this was not a disrespectful act. On the contrary, it was the only ethical, logical, and moral thing for them to do.

For Progressives, God, or at least the God of Conservative American Christians like us, is the enemy of all that is good, just, and fair in the world. Therefore, opposing God, and every vestige of Him in our society, is something all decent Progressives are committed to do, although some are less militant in their castigations than others. These fellow travelers may want God out of society, but they are not willing to be combative about it.

As patriotic Americans and committed Christians, in addition to being continuously shocked, saddened, outraged, and appalled by the actions of the Progressives, we are more confused by their worldview than anything. To us, it's inconceivable that people would want to dishonor God. That Progressives consider such disrespect as being moral is mindboggling.

Because the Progressive worldview is hostile to God and to Christianity, we have come to question them just as much as they do us.

Nevertheless, having had enough of their hostile contempt for our values and our American heritage, we are ready to fight back. Today, in the second decade of the twenty-first century, the battle lines between Progressivism and Christianity have been drawn, and they are crystal clear. The victor will determine the destiny for the United States of America for coming generations.

For us, this is a conflict worth waging and a battle worth fighting. Although patriotic Christian Americans have been moderately passive for generations, choosing to live our lives in peace, allowing "someone" else to fight the good fight, we can no longer afford to pursue our laissez-faire strategy of avoidance. If we do, all will be lost. Multiplied millions have come to realize that "leaving well enough alone" is a self-defeating strategy, and they are no longer willing to be passive.

Our time has come. We must make a stand. There is no other acceptable alternative, and the time to do it is now.

The Progressives have been waging societal war against us for many years, several generations in fact. They know the value of controlling government. To enforce their agenda, they must be in power. There is no acceptable alternative. So, anything that will gain them power, or keeps them in power, is moral, just, and right. Fairness is not part of their equation—not like it is for us.

To them, winning is everything, regardless of what it requires to achieve that goal.

They are consumed with enacting governmental regulations that will level the playing field—not just domestically but also internationally. For them, this is their consuming agenda. For us, by way of contrast, we prefer to just be left alone. Their goal is for the federal government to control every aspect of our lives. Our goal is for the federal government to have as little control over what we do as absolutely necessary. They want to engineer society through legal mandates that conform to establishing an open society, while we generally oppose any form of social engineering. We believe governmental mandates, which over-regulate our lives, are counterproductive to core American values, while they believe the exact opposite. For them, the more government we have the better off we will be.

Because the stakes are so high—the destiny of the United States—the societal conflicts between Progressivism and patriotic conservative Christians are sharp and profound. The Progressives, who are bolstered by the confidence they have in their intellectual superiority, are certain they will win this battle.

It is our job to make sure they don't. Unfortunately, many conservative Christians, having been intimidated by political correctness, tend to agree with them. Millions of believers actually believe the Progressives are destined to win this societal war.

Some, citing biblical prophecy, are convinced it is our destiny to lose to the Progressives. Choosing to forget that, "Greater is He who is in you, than he who is in the world," many Christians have come to believe our demise is inevitable—but this self-fulfilling prophecy is simply not true. In fact, it's the exact opposite.

We have acquiesced to the anti-Christian, anti-patriotic, and anti-privacy dictates of the Progressives for far too long. It's time for us to fight back, by standing together and appropriating the spiritual armor Almighty God has provided for us to wage war. Learning what this is and how to use it is precisely what *In God We Trust* is all about.

We are here to help. Together, having an impact throughout America, we will be active in our resistance to the godlessness of the Progressive worldview. To do this, it is imperative that we know more about what Progressives think and why.

To win a war of ideas, which is what we are fighting domestically, it's imperative that we know exactly what our opponents believe. We have already discussed this somewhat, but more needs to be thrashed out, especially how Progressives have revised American history to suit their purposes.

Essentially, the history they are teaching our children in school, as being accurate, has no foundation in the primary documents.

For them, the idea of self-evident truths and inalienable rights is archaic and devoid of value. These concepts are relics of the past, and they have no place in a post-modern society like twenty-first century America. To believe that these antiquated concepts have relevance is wrong thinking that doesn't even deserve serious consideration, so they don't value the truth of history.

That these concepts are foundational to the worldview of Conservative patriotic Christians, like us, shows them just how out of touch with reality fools like us really are.

The perspective of our forefathers, especially Christian thinkers, is rarely taken seriously. History has moved past the backwardness of our forefathers, which means there is little to learn from their opinions anyway. Besides, according to the Progressives, our forefathers were the ones who established slavery, raped the land, and were imperialistic robber barons.

We, on the other hand, disagree with this assessment. As patriotic Christians, we value the thinking and mindset of our founding fathers. They verbalized our core values. Their thinking is foundational to our Constitutional democracy and to the Rule of Law that binds us together as Americans. They articulated the intellectual groundwork to establish the Divinely given inalienable rights we cherish so dearly. Their inspired thought constitutes the foundation for the American way of life, and it should be honored—not rejected.

We wouldn't be who we are today without the philosophical contributions of our founding fathers. Their beliefs have made America free and safe. Because of them, not in spite of them, we are the greatest nation in the history of the world.

Because we believe this with all of our hearts, it is why we continue to insist that "originalists" be nominated for the Supreme Court. While Progressives want judges who believe the Constitution is a "living, breathing document," we want our heritage to be preserved.

They want judges who will interpret the Constitution, based on the prevailing values of the current culture that is dominated by them. What they insist upon is the exact opposite of what we want, which is why lifetime judicial appointments are so crucial to both sides.

In their minds, we are taking America backwards, which is completely unacceptable, from their perspective. What the Progressives want is a socialistic democracy, like many European nations have, but to achieve this would require a nearly complete repudiation of our traditional American value system. What Progressives desire horrifies us.

We treasure our foundational documents—the Constitution, the Bill of Rights, the Federalist Papers, and the Declaration of Independence. There's no question about that. We hold these documents in high esteem, but we value the Scriptures even more. For us, the Bible is God's infallible, inerrant Word, and its tenets, which are ageless, constitute absolute truth. What the Bible says is as accurate today as it was when it was written. For us, this will never change—thank God.

For a Progressive, there is no such thing as absolute truth. All truth is relative. So, if the Constitution and Declaration of Independence are archaic manuscripts, how much more so is the Bible, which is thousands of years older than our founding documents?

For the Progressive, the Bible has nothing to do with the world in which we live. To believe that it does is ridiculous and illogical. Those who adhere to its tenets and quote it as being authoritative are irrational. To take such people seriously, which includes nearly all of us, is absurd. This is why Progressives do not respect us and never will. Instead, they believe—firmly believe—that we richly deserve all of the contempt they are more than happy to heap upon our heads.

But that's not all. Because the belief system of patriotic Christians like us is backwards, and completely divorced from reality, they believe it is actually dangerous for people like us to hold office. We have no moral right to govern, even if we do win elections. Because our belief system is delusional, no progress can be made while we are in office. Being backward in our thinking, all we are capable of doing is creating a mess that Progressives are forced to undo when they return to power, which they believe is inevitable.

This is also why Progressives never welcome the will of the American people, when it goes against theirs. We are too stupid and too backward thinking to know what we really need or what is best for us. Only they, the Progressive elites, are capable of grasping what is in the best interest of the American people.

In many ways, we have mirror images of one another. Both sides believe they are right and that the other side is dead wrong. Like trying to mix oil and water, combining our worldviews cannot be done successfully. The Progressives, who dominate academia and the media, intend to enforce their will upon us, even when they are out of office. They use intimidation and political correctness to keep us quiet and, until lately, they have been very successful at exerting their will over us.

Bullying is the preferred weapon Progressives use to enforce the primacy of their values. Nobody is allowed to question their dictates. To do so can be emotionally quite painful. Consequently, most non-Progressives have chosen to keep their perspective to themselves and remain silent.

Until quite recently, more believers than not have been unwilling to voice their opposition to the beliefs of Progressivism. The personal attacks they experience have been so vicious that it is simply easier to remain silent, rather than subject oneself to verbal abuse.

Things are changing, however, and they are changing fast. It's obvious this is true. This is why we, at *In God We Trust,* are putting forth a concerted effort to unite Christians in opposition to the destructive doctrines of Progressivism.

We stand firmly for what we believe and the values we hold dear. Because there is strength in numbers, our task has been made much easier. In America, our numbers are legion. When we are united, and walking in the Lord's will, we are stronger than our Progressive opponents—much stronger.

When God is with us, who can stand against us? That we are capable of having a perspective like this is absurd to a Progressive, but that's okay. We know the truth.

They scoff at us and ridicule our belief that governmental control should be limited. Committed to doing the exact opposite, there can never be too much government, according to Progressives, and there should be very little Constitutional constraint on its power. They are so insistent on this that they fight our idea of limiting government tooth and nail, using the liberal courts to do so.

Government is the only vehicle capable of creating the kind of society Progressives desire. Since this is true, it requires them to be in power. Having control over society is an absolute necessity. According to them, no good thing can happen if they are not running our nation.

It's also why they are obstructionists, when they are in the minority. Being in control means the government can effectively regulate our lives through laws, regulations, and executive fiat. That we balk, when Progressives over-regulate our lives, is irrelevant. They don't care what we think.

Governmental constraints over us are a good thing from the Progressive perspective. This is why they oppose any

Constitutional restrictions on their power. They resist each and every attempt to diminish the authority of government. What they fight to impose we contest just as vehemently to deny.

We see the social engineering of the government as an abuse of power, a contradiction to our way of life, and an attempt to squelch or circumvent our inalienable rights. We view the expansion of governmental control as Big Brother sinking his tentacles into every aspect of our lives, which we loathe.

Such intrusiveness violates our Constitutional rights and our ability to live our lives as free men and women. To us, governmental overreach and societal engineering have become so pervasive and intrusive that we hardly recognize the nation of our youth. This is unacceptable. We are determined to stand our ground against the federal government violating our civil rights. Here is a specific prayer for us at *In God We Trust*. We hope it resonates in your heart just as strongly as it does in ours.

Father, Stand with Us Amid This Crooked and Perverse Generation

Please Join Us in the Following Prayer

Father, Lord God Almighty:
We come before You today on bended knee,
Because our hearts are troubled and sorrowful.
We are apprehensive about our nation's future.
In Your goodness to us, during the last election,
As our nation was about to go over the cliff,
You spared us from certain destruction,
By foiling the ambitions of the social elite—
Those who desire to remove You from the public arena.

Hearing our prayers, which were offered by many,
You honored them by stopping the cold-hearted schemes
Of those who mock Your Name and ridicule Your children.
In Your benevolence, You gave us another chance
To change our wicked ways
That have been so dishonoring to You.
Thank You for Your benevolence and for Your mercy to us,
Which we do not deserve,
But which You have granted graciously.
Believing restitution of all that is good was within our grasp,
We, Your children, were overjoyed with
The prospects for the future.

But now, our joy and our enthusiasm have been short-lived,
As a dark shadow has come over the United States.
Ominous clouds threaten to undo our legitimate victory.
The forces of darkness, led by desperate men and women,
Loathsome creatures who hate Your name,
While championing corruption and depravity,
Have joined forces
With Progressives to alter the will of the American people
And abrogate our voice,
Which produced an electoral landslide.
Do not allow their scheming and plotting to succeed, Father.
Foil their plots and refute their lies
So that the entire world will marvel.
Refuse to grant the desires of the arrogant, those who believe
Their godless voices should
Exercise dominion over the righteous.
Defeat them, Father—not because we are deserving—
But because You have been merciful to America for Your plan.
We ask this in the Name of Jesus Christ,
Our Lord, and Your Son,
Amen.

CHAPTER 3

Standing Firm
Against a False Goɑ

Then God spoke all these words, saying,
I am the LORD YOUR GOD, WHO
BROUGHT YOU OUT OF THE LAND OF EGYPT,
OUT OF THE HOUSE OF SLAVERY.

"You shall have no other gods before Me. You shall not make for
yourself an idol, or any likeness of what is in heaven above or on
the earth beneath or in the water under the earth. You shall not
worship them or serve them; for I, the LORD YOUR GOD, AM A JEAL-
OUS GOD, VISITING THE INIQUITY OF THE FATHERS ON THE CHILDREN,
ON THE THIRD AND THE FOURTH GENERATIONS OF THOSE WHO HATE
ME, BUT SHOWING LOVINGKINDNESS TO THOUSANDS, TO THOSE WHO
LOVE ME AND KEEP MY COMMANDMENTS" (Exodus 20:1-6, NAS).

As Christians who desire God's will for America, we are clearly at odds with our Progressive political opponents. As we see it, the direction in which they want to take the United States repudiates everything past generations of Americans have stood for, including many things for which patriots have bled and died.

To defeat the goals of the Progressives and prevent them from taking place, we must be strong, resourceful, and absolutely mitted to maintaining our biblical value system. Nothing short of a commitment as significant as this will be effective.

The original vision for our great nation was for America to be a "City on a Hill." If this purpose was good enough for our forefathers, and it was, it certainly is good enough for us. Having maintained this vision since the Puritans landed in Boston Harbor in 1629, this is what has made our nation the envy of the world for centuries.

A Personal Journey–Don Black

My mother's maiden name was Kelsey. She always told us that her father had emigrated from Ireland during the potato famine. So we grew up thinking that our family was a combination of German and Irish (what dad called "Shanty Irish"). Well, about five years ago, with the help of "Ancestry.com," I took on the challenge to research our family tree. I am so glad that I did because it gave me an entirely different story of the Kelsey family legacy.

My research pointed out that mom's dad had not been born in Ireland after all, but rather in Wisconsin. To add to the confusion, he wasn't Irish but English. I wondered how mom's story was so far off. I realized that her memories were patched together from secondhand stories she gathered in her early childhood.

You see, the Great Depression had caused her family to lose everything, including their dairy farm, which had been passed down for several generations. My mom's care was taken over by the state of Wisconsin, and at the age of four she was placed in an orphanage. So her telling about her family history really came from loose memories and an imagination fueled by the need for her to belong.

But the real story of Harriet Kelsey's family tree is one of courage, adventure, and the fight for Christian freedom.

Her ancestor, William Kelsey, was the first of the Kelsey clan in America. He was born in 1600, in Chelmsford, Essex County, England. It is located just northeast of London toward the sea. He was the son of George Kelsey Jr. and Elizabeth Hammond. William had two brothers, John and Henry.

Kelsey was a man of great faith and dedication. He, and his family, were members of St. Mary's Congregational Church in Chelmsford, England, where their pastor, the Rev. Thomas Hooker, gained acclaim for his messages declaring liberty and freedom against the established Church of England.

Those were days of great persecution for anyone who stood against the absolute power of the State's religion. Rev. Hooker and his congregation joined in the Separatist Movement that has since been labeled as Puritans. This activist group believed that the Church of England needed to separate itself from the National Church in all ways. They didn't call themselves Puritans; they saw their mission as being focused on the Bible and separated from the restrictions of state rules and religious regulations.

Rev. Hooker had been forced to flee the Church of England's persecution, with its threatened fines and imprisonment. His congregation, almost as a whole, moved to New England. The next year Pastor Hooker joined them.

My Grandfather Kelsey and his family were members of the church and prayerfully joined in this adventure in faith. At thirty-two years of age, he and his pregnant wife gathered together their four-year old son, Mark, and two-year old daughter, Bethia, to prepare for a sudden and dramatic change of life. William was a common workingman (I am not sure what his occupation was in England, but when he came to New England he raised livestock). He wasn't a wealthy man. In fact, in order to have the money to make this trip, he didn't have any other choice but to offer himself as an indentured servant. That means, in exchange for him and his family's transportation to this new land, he had to legally agree to become a slave to the Massachusetts Bay Colony for a number of years to repay the debt. Before the American Revolution, a staggering 80% of all immigrants from England came to the Colonies as indentured servants. His must have been a two-year agreement because records show that he was made a freedman on March 4, 1635.

The journey across the Atlantic was long and dangerous

On June 22, 1632, the *Lyon* sailed from London, financed by a group of Puritan settlers headed by John Winthrop. It was the first of 13 sailing ships in the Winthrop fleet that embarked to New England that year. John Winthrop (1587-1649) was a wealthy Puritan lawyer and a leading figure in the founding of the Massachusetts Bay Colony, the first major settlement in New England after Plymouth Colony.

The ship was larger and more comfortable than the Mayflower (which proved unfit for another voyage, after the famous trip in 1620 carrying the Pilgrim Fathers). It is known that the captain's name was William Pierce and that the Lyon sailed from London about the 22nd of June, 1632. It arrived in Boston on Sunday, the 16th of September, following after a voyage of eight weeks from Landsend, although the passengers had been aboard for twelve weeks. They had five days of east wind and fog, but no disaster. There were one hundred and twenty-three passengers of which fifty were children, all in good health. According to the records, there were sixty men on the *Lyon*, and as fifty were children, the rest must have been wives and other women. Many were related or became related by marriage. Henry Adams and family were aboard. (His family tree produced two U.S. presidents.)

On arrival to the Massachusetts Bay Colony, they "begin to sit down" at Mount Hollingston, a few miles from Boston; but it being the policy of the Colony to keep the population as concentrated as possible, the court ordered them to change locations.

My ancestor, William Kelsey, was one of the original "Braintree

Company" followers of the Reverend Thomas Hooker, who came to America. They were the first settlers of "New Towne" (now Cambridge), Massachusetts in 1632. Reverend Hooker joined them there a year later.

Another move for freedom

Life in the Colony was divided between several factions. It was a very controlled society led by pious men of newfound wealth. The region was exploding with new immigrants and the need to expand the Colony. I find it interesting that a year after my ancestor Kelsey earned his freedom, he decided to pick up and move his growing family again—now with three girls, one boy, and his wife again pregnant.

In June of 1636, Rev. Hooker and a Mr. Stone, with more than 50 other families of the "first church" moved again—this time to Connecticut, where in the valley of the same name, they established another "New Towne" (which was later changed to Hartford). The "Company" remained there until 1663 when they again picked up and moved to establish another "New Towne" that was later named Killingworth, Connecticut. It was here that William stayed until his death in 1680.

He lived quite an exciting life. He fathered ten children and helped to birth this new land. William Kelsey's name appears on the "founders monument" in the "ancient burying ground" of the First Congregational Church, currently known as Center Church. His name appears as one of the twenty-five men on the "Adventurer's Boulder," which is located at City Hall in Hartford, Connecticut. The plaque reads "*In memory of the courageous adventurers who, inspired and directed by Thomas Hooker, journeyed through the wilderness from Newtown (Cambridge) in the Massachusetts Bay to Suckiauc (Hartford).*"

These men, with their families, began a journey in search of personal freedom when they left England as a church body, and their long journey for freedom ended in the river valley of Connecticut.

They banded together with two other cities and created a written compact upon which they would base their personal lives and communities. That agreement was named the Fundamental Orders.

The Connecticut Council adopted the Fundamental Orders on January 15, 1639. It describes a government that was established by the Connecticut River towns, setting its structure, limits, and powers.

The Orders had the features of a constitution, and is considered the first written constitution in the western tradition—it so earned Connecticut its nickname, "The Constitution State."

There is no record of the debates, proceedings of the drafting, or enactment of the Fundamental Orders. It is suggested that its framers wished to remain anonymous to avoid retaliation by the English authorities.

According to historian John Taylor, *"The men of the three towns were a law unto themselves. It is known that they were in earnest for the establishment of a government on broad lines and it is certain that the ministers and captains, the magistrates and men of affairs, forceful in the settlements from the beginning, were the men who took the lead, guided the discussions. Together they founded the root of the whole matter in the first written Declaration of Independence in these historical orders."*

It took brave families like my ancestor William Kelsey's to begin to carve a Republic out of the wilderness of the new America. They came for one primary cause, to be allowed to worship and live as free men. This was the Spirit that made America the greatest nation in world history.

As hundreds of millions of Americans are wise enough to still realize, we must continue to remain in the flow of God's original blessing. This is also why we remain as strong as we are in the twenty-first century. Recognizing our founder's original goal, it is our purpose, at *In God We Trust,* to refocus our vision on the core values that made America great and safe. We believe this resolve will make us even greater in the future.

But it will not be easy. Nothing of lasting value ever is. Clearly, we have opponents from within, but they are not our mortal enemies. The Progressives are just misguided citizens—people who have bought the lie that more government is the solution to all of our problems.

More than anything, they are to be pitied. Professing to be wise, they have become fools (Romans 1:22), but they are still Americans. We may be exasperated with them, but our conflict is fraternal. It's over ideas, leadership, and direction. Our combat is verbal—a battle of wills. Although they are formidable, Progressivism isn't our worst foe—far from it.

There is another threat, an external one that is being waged with weapons of terror. Although only a few realize it—despite continued attacks, producing many casualties—the primary conflict is about ideology and about how each side views spiritual reality. This clash involves fanatical belief in a false god. Therefore, our battle, our nation's life and death struggle, is with Radical Islam.

To be sure, there are nation-states who also wish to harm America, like Russia and North Korea, but historically, there have always been nations who have wanted to destroy us. Our conflicts with them have been much more clear-cut and easy to define than the battle we are now facing.

Our war is with Radical Islamic Terrorism, which imposes a threat unlike anything we have ever had to deal with. Nothing has even come close to approximating the struggle we are now facing, and we are not doing as well as we must.

Precisely like our conflict with the Progressives, there has to be a winner, and there has to be a loser. Where Radical Islam is concerned, however, our conflict is a zero sum game for national survival. The Jihadists want to destroy the United States. The Progressives just want to change our nation into something that we never have been.

Radical Islamists consider us to be the "Great Satan." Because we are of the devil, their goal is to subjugate all Americans, including Progressives, and force us to worship their god, Allah.

As Christians, as well as being patriotic Americans, this is something none of us would ever be willing to do. Just the thought of it is inconceivable. Nevertheless, we must take the threat of Radical Islam seriously, which the last President seemed not to do. Time has proven this was a mistake by the Obama administration—a serious mistake—but it is something that must be rectified.

At *In God We Trust*, with the help of Almighty God and people like you, we intend to stand strong for our beliefs and for the United States of America. We know exactly what Radical Islam is and what their goals are. This is why we intend to confront with truth the false belief system of this errant political religion head on.

To be effective, we need to understand the worldview of Islam— just like we need to be wise about the Progressive belief system. Without understanding the mindset of Progressivism, we will never be able to put America back on track. In the same way, we must understand the mindset of Radical Islamists, and it begins by taking what they say seriously.

To think that Jihadism is a minor problem, like the Obama administration did for eight years (never even being willing to acknowledge its existence), is an egregious mistake.

We recognize that Radical Islam has been at war with the rest of the world for centuries. After Mohammed's death in 632, the new Muslim caliph, Abu Bakr, launched Islam into almost 1,500 years of continual imperialist, colonialist, bloody conquest and subjugation of others through invasion and war, a role Islam continues to this very day.

America's conflict with Radical Islam began as early as the late 1700s, when pirates from Tripoli raided American cargo ships and held them for ransom. They did this with many other nations to fund their expansion. It wasn't until 1804, when recently elected President Thomas Jefferson declared war and sent our newly formed navy to defeat them. Interestingly, this is where the lyric from the Marine Corp Hymn, "From the shores of Tripoli," originated.

Our generation may remember when Ayatollah Khomeini seized the U.S. Consulate in Tehran in 1979. But in the minds of most Americans, the conflict with Radical Islam came home when terrorists hijacked four jet planes on 9/11/2001, crashing them into the Twin Towers in New York, the Pentagon in Washington

DC. We remember the bravery of the passengers on United Airlines Flight 93 to sacrificially bring down their hijacked plane in a strip mine in Pennsylvania.

From that day forward, nearly every thinking American—those who were willing to see the world as it was—knew for certain that we had a serious problem on our hands. After the shock of 9/11, this was when we decided to fight back in earnest, and freedom-loving Americans have been waging war ever since.

Progressives tend to dismiss or underestimate the threat of Islamic terrorism. They consider it to be a minor problem. After all, they reason, in order to appease worried Americans like us, terrorists represent just a small percentage of Islam. To further placate us, they repeatedly maintain that Islam is really a "Religion of Peace."

Nobody knows for certain exactly how many Islamic Terrorists there are. Some maintain that the percentage of radicals is as high as 10 percent. Others believe it is as small as 1 percent. While these percentages of the total Muslim population in the world are low, because of the number of Muslims there are, the quantity of radicals is actually staggeringly high. That's because there are estimated to be 1.5 billion Muslims in the world.

This means that if 10 percent are radical, there are 150 million Muslim Jihadists. To put this number into perspective, it equates to more than all of the men, women, and children who live in Russia, and it seems that all the secular media can talk about is the possible threat of Russian collusion.

If the smaller number is more accurate, and just 1 percent has been radicalized, it still equates to a large number of people. Fifteen million represents slightly more than all of the people who live in the state of Pennsylvania—men, women, and children. So, it's obvious there are significantly more Jihadists than we have been led to believe.

This makes Radical Islam a real and present danger to the United States of America. Because the threat is so significant, it is a problem that must be addressed. To do so effectively, however, we need to understand exactly what they believe concerning global conquest. To defeat an enemy, one must know who the enemy is. Understanding what Radical Islam is, and calling it out for what it is, remains our number one security issue.

That the Progressives have refused to take the threat of Radical Islam seriously has put the United States in a difficult position. Refusing to take a firm stand against Radical Islam has made us unnecessarily vulnerable. Thankfully, we are no longer being led by the naive policies of idealistic Progressives who force reality to conform to their flawed ideology.

As patriotic Christians, and people who have the ability to discern the truth, we understand that the nature of America's conflict with Radical Islam is rooted in a spiritual dimension. In addition to our military conflict with ISIS, al Qaeda, and the Taliban, we are also engaged with Islam in spiritual warfare. Few are willing to acknowledge this, but it is true. There are physical and spiritual wars occurring simultaneously.

It is our Commander-in-Chief's responsibility, along with his generals, to fight Radical Islamic Terrorism in the physical realm, but it is our job, as believers, to wage war in the spiritual realm. To fight the good fight effectively, we must be crystal clear about the worldview that Radical Islam is willing to die for. Half measures will avail us nothing. By necessity, we must call a spade a spade.

To begin with, Allah is a false god. He demands that his adherents submit to his will. To be perfectly frank, Islam is a religion of subjugation. There is no grace in Islam whatsoever. To be a submissive Muslim, Allah demands that his followers die for him.

In truth, Islam is the exact opposite of Christianity. Muslims must die for Allah, while our God died for us. The difference couldn't be clearer or more stark.

Concerning our American heritage, our way of life has evolved from our traditional Christian value system. You cannot accurately comprehend the history of the United States without having a deep understanding of our Christian origins.

Historically, faith has been an essential ingredient in everything we have done, or attempted to do. It has been this way since the time of the Pilgrims and the Puritans in the early seventeenth century, and their beliefs go back to the origin of the Judeo-Christian Ethic in the first century.

If this is true of us, then the same is true for Muslims. One cannot understand who they are without recognizing that their faith in Allah, which began in the seventh century, determines their worldview. We want freedom to worship God in peace, while they want their beliefs to dominate every aspect of their lives. The difference is this: they don't just want this for themselves, but they also insist upon it for the lives of everybody else in the world.

Their goal is to create a worldwide Caliphate. In their belief system, this is somewhat similar to what Christians are waiting for; the thousand-year millennial reign of Christ. This Caliphate is what they intend to produce, and they are willing to die to make it become a reality. Some want this so much they are willing to crash a plane into a building or strap a bomb to their bodies and blow up dozens of innocent people, just to create fear in those who survive their suicide.

Obviously, they are willing to die for their cause, but they are not insane. They are just committed to their false god and are willing to martyr themselves to create his Caliphate.

Sharia Law defines the foundation for the Muslim way of life. Rigid adherence to its tenets is required, but not all Muslims are as militant as the Radical Jihadists. In fact, most Muslims are no more religious than most who identify as being Christian.

Nevertheless, it is the overwhelming belief of Muslims that their way of life and Sharia Law must supplant the Rule of Law and our Constitution. For them, there is no compromise about this, and there can be no middle ground. Sharia Law must prevail. There is only one way, their way.

This is why Radical Islamic immigrants refuse to assimilate like other ethnic minorities have done in America for centuries. Peaceful coexistence isn't even a consideration for them. It's not on their radar—not long-term anyway. They must dominate, and Sharia Law must become the law of the land in the United States— not the United States Constitution. It is a religion of peace, and they define peace as the absence or subjugation of infidels. An infidel is anyone that doesn't believe the way they believe. To this they are committed and to think otherwise, just because it fits the Progressive narrative, is foolhardy and dangerous.

Unfortunately, most Americans do not grasp the magnitude of this simple truth, but this is what differentiates Islam from other ethnic minorities who want to assimilate into the American way of life. Radical Islamists are determined to nullify our Constitutional system of government and make America and the rest of the world conform to the uncompromising dictates of Islam's Sharia Law. That this is what they intend to produce isn't even given credence as being important. These core Islamic convictions are rarely even taken into consideration by enlightened Progressives, naive that they are.

In fact, there is a popular belief among Progressives that everybody wants socialistic democracy, individual freedom, and equality under the law. This is a fundamental desire for Mankind, according to Progressives. They believe that, if only Radical Muslims could be educated about democratic ideas, they would overwhelmingly embrace our superior way of life. That we are the "Great Satan" doesn't even compute to the Progressive way of thinking. They consider such rhetoric to be unimportant and irrelevant, which Muslims certainly do not.

To Progressives, Radical Islamic Terrorists are the way they are because they haven't been given a legitimate chance in life. Terrorists behave the way they do because of poverty, corrupt dictatorial governments, and a lifetime of abuse. Some Progressives even blame terrorism on global warming.

They reason that, since the world is getting hotter, the Middle East is becoming increasingly uninhabitable. Therefore, it is only natural that these poor unfortunate Middle Eastern Muslims would want to find new places to live, and since all they know is war, it's the only way they know how to get what they need… poor, misunderstood terrorists.

Wanting to find a more temperate climate, this is why they have moved to Europe, where they are becoming a dominant political force. Now, they are targeting the United States, where they intend to dominate us as well.

The only reason they are violent, according to Progressives, is because they haven't been given a legitimate chance in life. All they have ever known is inequality, so it's only natural that they would finally become so frustrated that they would lash out.

Recently, there was a news report on network television that featured a young lady who was carrying a large poster board that proudly proclaimed her answer to global terror.

It simply stated in large letters: GIVE ISIS A HUG!

This ridiculous, nonsensical, and historically inaccurate thinking isn't the exclusive domain of Progressives, however. Millions of non-Progressives also believe this nonsense is true.

Ever since the United States was successful at establishing democracies in Germany and Japan at the end of World War II, after both nations had been dominated by totalitarian regimes before the war, the United States has been in the business of nation building. Despite how successful we were in the post-War era with Germany and Japan, and South Korea after the Korean Conflict, we have never been able to fully replicate our nation's success. Nevertheless, like the Energizer Bunny, we keep trying, hoping to find a natural solution for a spiritual problem.

In the Middle East, our attempts have been particularly disastrous. Our efforts to produce democracies out of Iraq, Afghanistan, Libya, and even Egypt, have all failed miserably. Essentially, other than our steadfast support for the constitutional democracy in Israel, for over a half-century, our foreign policy in the Middle East has been misguided, producing nothing but repeated disappointments.

There's a reason for this. Ignorantly, we have failed to make the tenets of Islam as part of the equation in our Middle Eastern foreign policy. Instead, we have consistently underestimated the depth of the Islamic belief system, particularly where political ideology is involved. This failure has cost us dearly, and we hope that it doesn't continue.

Because we foolishly believe Radical Muslims are fundamentally like us, which they are not, we have failed to deal with them, especially where radicalism in the Middle East is so prevalent, for what Islam really is. Islam is not just a religion; it is also a life-consuming totalitarian ideology. You cannot separate its religious component from its political agenda, but this is exactly what we have done. The two are forever joined together.

This is why Progressives, who have a secular ideology, can never stop the encroachment of Islam in America. Progressives not only fail to understand the power of Islam's religious component, but they are also incapable of fathoming the motivational power this belief system has on its adherents.

Muslims have not been radicalized by global warming or poverty—far from it. They are motivated to radical behavior because it is the will of their god, Allah. He wants them to subjugate the infidels, especially the Great Satan, by Jihad. Since we are the heathen, Allah has called faithful Muslims to conquer us. We must understand what motivates these people; accept it for what it is, and address the problem it creates appropriately.

Since the seventh century, when Muslims first became a political threat, it has been Christianity that has stopped Islam from dominating the world. In the twenty-first century, this task has fallen upon Christianity again. Although we didn't ask for this assignment, it has become our responsibility—at least the spiritual dynamic.

This is why we at *In God We Trust*, intend to bring together millions of Christians nationwide to pray and fast for our nation. America must lead the world in pushing back the threat of Radical Islam, and we must be at the forefront of this effort. It was rewarding to witness President Trump's first international trip in the spring of 2017 to Saudi Arabia. They convened at a conference with more than fifty Arab and Muslim leaders, all of whom agreed to combat Radical Islamic terror together. This was a landmark meeting that is a first step to end terror's deadly grip on the West.

What we need to do is every bit as important, and as effective, as any military operation proposed by the Pentagon and approved by our Commander-in-Chief.

Our God, the Father of our Lord, Jesus Christ, is real and He is Almighty. Allah, by way of contrast, may be a spiritual being, but he is certainly not god, nor is he almighty.

Our God Reigns,
Not Their False God

Please Join Us in the Following Prayer

Father, Lord God, Almighty,
As a nation, despite our vast expanse and wide oceans
That act as giant moats protecting us East and West,
In our arrogant foolishness,
We have taken our safety for granted.
Casting aside prudence for a worldview that refuses to accept
The true nature of Man, we have been steadily racing
Headlong away from comprehending reality
Or the true nature of those who wish to destroy us.
Believing a lie, while consistently disregarding the truth,
We have planted and nourished
The seeds of our self-destruction.
Although the world is dangerous, until the disaster of 9/11,
We refused to recognize the truth, while championing a lie,
Which we can no longer afford to do—
Not and expect to survive.

Radical Islamic fundamentalists intend to destroy our nation
And subjugate the American people,
Forcing us to worship their false god.
In the foolishness of our hearts,
We have not taken this threat

As seriously as we should have, but now we do.
We recognize that it is our responsibility,
As believers in Jesus Christ
To be salt to our nation and light to a dark and fallen world.
Instead of sitting idly by, hoping that others will lead the way,
We acknowledge that this responsibility belongs to us.
We must take it seriously and act accordingly,
But we cannot do this on our own—
Not and achieve the victory.

We need Your wisdom, guidance, and strength
To lead the way. Without You, all of our efforts
Will fail, and our beloved nation will suffer the consequences.
Be with us, embolden and empower us to stand strong.
Allow us to be as courageous as our founding fathers,
Who committed their lives and fortunes to create
The land of the free and the home of the brave.

In Your strength, Father, we trust that You will stand with us,
We march boldly into the future to confront
The false god of Islam and the false tenets of Sharia Law.
By faith, we commit our cause to You and ask that
You honor our purpose, protect us, and keep our nation safe.
We ask this in the name of
Your only begotten Son, Jesus Christ,
Amen.

CHAPTER 4

The Historical Tradition of Christianity in America

You are the light of the world. A city set on a hill cannot be hidden
(Matthew 5:14, NAS).

Just as we cannot understand the purpose and goals of Radical Islamic Terrorism without understanding the nature of Islam, neither can we understand our American way of life without knowing our Christian origins. It simply isn't possible to do this and be historically accurate.

The Progressives, under the guise of separation of church and state, have done everything within their considerable power to secularize American history, going so far as to state that Thanksgiving originated as a day when the Pilgrims gave thanks to the Indians rather than to Almighty God.

When President Obama said that Islam has been part of the fabric of American history since the beginning, he was not challenged by the mainstream media about his statement being historically inaccurate.

There's a reason he wasn't. It's because his assertion fits the narrative that the Progressives want to believe about America.

To remain true to the vision of our founding fathers, which was to be a "city on a hill" for the entire world to see, we must not allow the Progressives to redefine American history to suit their purposes. In their revisionism, Progressives have not only repudiated the role of Almighty God, but they have also scoffed at the idea we still revere God and depend on His leadership daily. To Progressives, prayer is not only nonsensical; it is also offensive because it is a repudiation of their worldview, which is almost completely material.

They would love to deny God's role in American history completely, but they can't. The reason they can't is because the historical record will not allow them to do so. It is filled with documents showing how our founding fathers, and the Presidents who followed them, repeatedly sought God's will for America.

Since we know this is true, it is incumbent upon us to stand for the truth our heritage represents and not allow the historical revisionism of the Progressives to go unchecked.

As stated earlier by the British Parliamentarian Edmund Burke in the eighteenth century, "The only thing necessary for Evil to triumph is for good men to do nothing." Being good men and women, who are faithful to God and love our country, we have no intention of standing by idly, while our enemies from within and from without do everything they can to weaken and destroy our beloved nation. This is why we are taking a stand, a firm stand, for God and country.

Our goal is to help men and women of faith unite through the power of prayer and fasting. Our purpose is to transform this great nation of ours, by bringing America back into alignment with our traditional Judeo-Christian value system. This is what is required to make America great and safe again.

We know this is true: "Greater is He who is in you than he who is in the world" (1 John 4:4). Bolstered by this conviction, we intend to confront the false god of the Radical Islamic Terrorists, as well as the equally false beliefs of American Progressives—those who are attacking America from within, by imposing their anti-American and anti-theistic worldview on our children and grandchildren. With your help, we can and will make a difference.

Historically, before political correctness was dominant, Presidents were very forthright about their faith, going so far as to call for prayer often. Doing so has been a long, respected tradition in the United States. But because of the militancy of the radical, anti-theistic, Progressive Left, asking Almighty God to favor us and keep us safe from harm is no longer in vogue. For the most part, it has fallen into disuse.

At *In God We Trust*, we intend to do everything we can to resurrect this tradition.

For instance, the last time a President made a Proclamation similar to the one we have proposed was during the administration of President Woodrow Wilson. He was our 28th President and a Democrat from New Jersey. Guiding America through The Great War, which did not become known as World War I until the beginning of World War II, President Wilson fully understood the value of calling upon all Americans to pray and fast to Almighty God, asking for the forgiveness of our national sins and our many shortcomings.

Wilson made his Proclamation, asking for prayer, fasting, and repentance, ninety-nine years ago. What he referred to in the Proclamation as "humiliation" now equates more accurately to what we call repentance. Here is Wilson's Proclamation 1445:

"Now, Therefore, I, Woodrow Wilson, President of the United States of America, do hereby proclaim Thursday, the thirtieth day of May, a day already freighted with sacred and stimulating memories, a day of public humiliation, prayer, and fasting, and do exhort my fellow-citizens of all faiths and creeds to assemble on that day in their several places of worship and there, as well as in their homes, to pray Almighty God that He may forgive our sins and shortcomings as a people and purify our hearts to see and love the truth, to accept and defend all things that are just and right, and to purpose only those righteous acts and judgments which are in conformity with His will; beseeching Him that He will give victory to our armies as they fight for freedom, wisdom to those who take counsel on our behalf in these days of dark struggle and perplexity, and steadfastness to our people to make sacrifices to the utmost in support of what is just and true, bringing us at last the peace in which men's hearts can be at rest because it is founded upon mercy, justice and good will.

"In Witness Whereof, I have hereunto set my hand and caused the seal of the United States to be affixed.

"Done in the District of Columbia this eleventh day of May, in the year of our Lord Nineteen hundred and eighteen and of the independence of the United States the one hundred and forty-second."

Wilson's Proclamation is the precedent we claim and the model we are following, but it certainly isn't the only historical example we could have used of a national leader calling for prayer. There have been many times in our history, when one of our Presidents has prayed publicly to Almighty God, asking all Americans to join him in his effort.

Unfortunately, millions of Americans, especially our younger generations, have no idea how instrumental prayer and fasting have been as vehicles our leaders used in times of crisis to determine our nation's direction. This shouldn't be surprising though. After all, the extraordinary responsibility and awesome power of each Chief Executive relentlessly drove the wiser ones to their knees.

Maybe it's because our younger generation has been indoctrinated with historical revisionism, rather than historical facts, that they have no knowledge of the role of prayer from our national leaders. Unfortunately, to make them more susceptible to Progressive ideology, our impressionable youth have come to believe America was founded on secular values.

According to most Progressives, the role of Christianity in the founding and establishing of the United States was minor, at best. Being taught this in school, being young and naive, our kids and grandkids have accepted what they are taught as the true report—but it isn't. Our founders were people of faith, whose core convictions were guided by their belief in God.

Recent administrations have gone out of their way to minimize the role of Christianity in America's founding, in a calculated assault on people of faith. Unfortunately, millions of millennials have accepted this historical revisionism as true. They steadfastly maintained that America is not a Christian nation. Because they continue to proclaim this ideology, many Americans have accepted this concept as being accurate, but nothing could be further from the truth. This version of American history is either misinformed or is purposefully deceptive by design.

There is also a position proclaimed that Islam was an integral part of the fabric of America and has been since our inception. That Islam helped build this great nation is a naive assertion that is definitely not historically accurate. Other than Thomas Jefferson, our third President, having a copy of the Quran in his library, there is no historical evidence to support any misleading assertion about the role of Islam—none whatsoever.

There isn't a shred of proof to support this nonsensical assertion, but millions of Americans believe it's true. Not surprisingly, secular journalism has never challenged this revisionist perspective.

In dispute of these history-altering assertions, there is a mountain of historical evidence (including primary documents) that clearly demonstrate how significant Christianity was to earlier generations. In fact, many public prayers that were uttered by our founding fathers are part of our historical record.

The biblical values that Christians like you and I cherish today are the same ones that were espoused by patriotic Christians two centuries ago. It's important to know that our beliefs have been fervently maintained and proclaimed by a "great cloud of witnesses" from past generations of Americans. Nevertheless, the politically correct have done their best to stifle the truth, as well as the historical evidence—all in an effort to institutionalize their lies, in an effort to propagandize our youth.

Fearing the vicious verbal abuse of the Left, millions of Christians—peaceful, gentle people of faith—have chosen to remain silent rather than object, but we can no longer be silent. We have remained in the shadows for too long without making the kind of stand for righteousness our forefathers did generations earlier.

Millions of them fought, and many of them bled and died, just to preserve the rights we have today. These are the same rights the Progressive Left now wants to discard, but we are not going to allow this to happen. It's our turn, as patriotic Christians, to stand and be counted.

It's time for us to be faithful to God, exactly the way so many other Americans have been from earlier generations. To be the most effective we can be, however, it's imperative that we have a firm grasp on our historical roots. By knowing the truth, we will not be susceptible to the deceitfulness of the Progressive viewpoint.

This is why we have included several instances in our history for you to read, where prayer to Almighty God was significant. You can see for yourself what happened in the past. Based on this information, we are adding historical context. This will let you know that our mission is consistent with what our Founding Fathers valued in the beginning and continued to cherish in subsequent generations.

Prayer for America's Future

Please Join Us in the Following Prayer

Father, Lord God Almighty,
Our hearts are heavy and deeply troubled.
We have a dreadful foreboding for the future.
After benefitting from the rewards of Your blessings
For generations, it seems like the path we are following,
Which the Progressives have set for us,
Will end in national heartache, disgrace, and destruction.
Throughout our history, millions have honored You,
Acknowledging that You are the source of everything
Good and honorable that we have enjoyed,
But this is no longer true. As a people,
We no longer honor You or give thanks.

In fact, we do the exact opposite. Now, we are being led
By Progressive elites who mock Your name—
Those who champion
A way that is contrary to the ways of our forefathers.
In their devious hearts, these reprobates hold
Your people in contempt, calling us
Deplorable and irredeemable.
Spurred by the media, who speak with serpentine tongues,
They champion wrong and call it right,
Congratulating themselves

For being enlightened, but they are not. They are deceived.
Tragically, they persuade many of our children to accept
The ways of darkness, calling them wise and beneficial.

We deserve the destruction that is heading our way.
There can be no doubt about that, but in Your graciousness,
You can spare us from the onslaught of
Progressivism's deceitfulness.
You are slow to anger, gracious, and quick to forgive.
For the sake of those of us who have made a stand for You,
Please spare our nation—not because we deserve to be spared,
Which we do not, but because of
Your boundless lovingkindness.
We ask this in the name of
Your Son and our Lord Jesus Christ,
Amen.

CHAPTER 5

Our Forefathers
Sought God's Will

Blessed is the man who perseveres under trial; for once he has been approved, he will receive the crown of life, which the Lord has promised to those who love Him,
(James 1:12, NAS).

I love to study history! This chapter partially fascinates me because it is largely based on the research of one of America's great historians, William Federer. He has enumerated and explained American history, going back to before the Revolution, based on the historical documents. As you study, it will help you to know that the values we hold so dear have unshakable roots in American history.

In 1774, after the British blockaded Boston Harbor, Thomas Jefferson drafted a *Resolution for the Colonists.* He called for a Day of Fasting, Humiliation and Prayer. Robert Carter Nicholas introduced this resolution in the Virginia House of Burgesses. With the support of Patrick Henry, Richard Henry Lee, and George Mason, it passed unanimously. The Resolution said in part:

> This House, being deeply impressed with apprehension of the great dangers, to be derived to British America, from the hostile invasion of the City of Boston, in our sister Colony of Massachusetts... deem it highly necessary that the said first day of June be set apart, by the members of this House as a Day of Fasting, Humiliation, and Prayer, devoutly to implore the Divine interposition, for averting the heavy calamity which threatens destruction to our civil rights... Ordered, therefore that the Members of this House do attend... with the Speaker, and the Mace, to the Church in this City, for the purposes aforesaid; and that the Reverend Mr. Price be appointed to read prayers, and the Reverend Mr. Gwatkin, to preach a sermon.

This seminal resolution had far-reaching implications. In fact, this day of prayer, fasting, and humiliation led to the forming of the first Continental Congress.

As you can see, seeking the will of God, and following it, was firmly engrained in the minds and hearts of our founding fathers. Just four days before the Battle of Lexington (which is just sixteen miles outside of Boston), on April 15, 1775, John Hancock declared the following:

> In circumstances dark as these, it becomes us, as men and Christians, to reflect that, whilst every prudent measure should be taken to ward off the impending judgments... the 11th of May next be set apart as a

Day of Public Humiliation, Fasting, and Prayer… to confess the sins… to implore the Forgiveness of all our Transgressions.

As the idea of becoming independent from the British Empire gained momentum, so did the need to be certain it was God's will. On April 19, 1775, speaking about the Proclamation of a Day of Fasting and Prayer, Connecticut Governor Jonathan Trumbull expressed the need of the Colonists to seek God's will. He asked that:

God would graciously pour out His Holy Spirit on us to bring us to a thorough repentance and effectual reformation that our iniquities may not be our ruin; that He would restore, preserve and secure the liberties of this and all the other British American colonies, and make the land a mountain of Holiness, and habitation of righteousness forever.

Once expressed, these ideas found fertile soil in the hearts of the Colonists. Reeling from the implications of conflict with England, less than two months after the Battles of Lexington and Concord (where "the shot heard 'round the world" was fired), John Hancock, President of the Continental Congress, declared:

Congress… considering the present critical, alarming and calamitous state… do earnestly recommend, that Thursday, the 12th of July next, be observed by the inhabitants of all the English Colonies on this Continent, as a Day of Public Humiliation, Fasting, and Prayer, that we may with united hearts and voices, unfeignedly confess and deplore our many sins and offer up our joint supplications to the All-wise, Omnipotent and merciful Disposer of all Events, humbly beseeching Him to forgive our iniquities... It is recommended to Christians of all denominations to assemble for public worship and to abstain from servile labor and recreations of said day.

The idea spread rapidly throughout the Colonies, reaching Georgia on July 5, 1775. Just a year before the Declaration of Independence, the Georgia Provincial Congress passed a motion, which affirmed: "A motion... that this Congress apply to his Excellency the Governor... requesting him to appoint a Day of Fasting and Prayer throughout this Province, on account of the disputes subsisting between America and the Parent State."

A little over a week later, on July 12, 1775, in a letter to his wife, John Adams wrote, "We have appointed a Continental fast. Millions will be upon their knees at once before their great Creator, imploring His forgiveness and blessing; His smiles on American Council and arms."

To rebel against the legitimate King of England was treason, which our founding fathers knew quite well, but they also believed that pursuing Colonial independence was the will of God. Being

firmly committed to becoming a free and indep
the need to interpret and follow God's will b
important thing in the world to our founding fathe₁₃.
their justification for sedition and establishing an army to fight
the British Red Coats.

It wasn't just the political leaders who spent time on their knees.
The general of the Continental Army, George Washington, did
as well. He ordered his men to pray. While in his Cambridge
headquarters, near Boston, Washington ordered that March,
16, 1776, be set apart: "[A]s a Day of Fasting, Prayer, and
Humiliation, to implore the Lord and Giver of all victory to
pardon our manifold sins and wickedness, and that it would
please Him to bless the Continental army with His divine favor
and protection, all officers and soldiers are strictly enjoined to
pay all due reverence and attention on that day to the sacred
duties to the Lord of hosts for His mercies already received, and
for those blessings which our holiness and uprightness of life can
alone encourage us to hope through His mercy obtain."

Once the political leaders and the Continental Army were
seeking God's will for the move for independence, the colonists
themselves were also asked. So, on March 16, 1776, the
Continental Congress passed a resolution declaring:

> Congress… desirous… to have people of all ranks and
> degrees duly impressed with a solemn sense of God's
> superintending providence, and of their duty, devoutly

to rely... on his aid and direction... do earnestly recommend Friday, the 17th day of May be observed by the colonies as a Day of Humiliation, Fasting, and Prayer; that we may, with united hearts, confess and bewail our manifold sins and transgressions, and, by sincere repentance and amendment of life, appease God's righteous displeasure, and, through the merits and mediation of Jesus Christ, obtain this pardon and forgiveness.

The colonists were not just asked to pray, fast, and repent. Their purpose was to discover God's will about their desire to seek independence. Additionally, they asked God for victory on the battlefield. Specifically, on May 15, 1776, General George Washington ordered:

The Continental Congress having ordered Friday the 17th to be observed as a Day of Fasting, Humiliation, and Prayer, humbly to supplicate the mercy of Almighty God, that it would please Him to pardon all our manifold sins and transgressions, and to prosper the arms of the United Colonies, and finally establish the peace and freedom of America upon a solid and lasting foundation; the General commands all officers and soldiers to pay strict obedience to the orders of the Continental Congress; that, by their unfeigned and pious observance of their religious duties, they may incline the Lord and Giver of victory to prosper our arms.

Having miraculously survived a bitterly cold winter at Valley Forge, once spring arrived (out of gratitude for surviving) on April 12, 1778, General Washington ordered:

> The Honorable Congress having thought proper to recommend to the United States of America to set apart Wednesday, the 22nd, to be observed as a day of Fasting, Humiliation, and Prayer, that at one time, and with one voice, the righteous dispensations of Providence may be acknowledged, and His goodness and mercy towards our arms supplicated and implored: The General directs that the day shall be most religiously observed in the Army; that no work shall be done thereon, and that the several chaplains do prepare discourses.

Later, on November 11, 1779, as Governor of Virginia, Thomas Jefferson signed a proclamation that stated:

> Congress... hath thought proper... to recommend to the several States... a day of publick and solemn Thanksgiving to Almighty God, for his mercies, and of Prayer, for the continuance of his favour... That He would go forth with our hosts and crown our arms with victory; that He would grant to His church, the plentiful effusions of Divine Grace, and pour out His Holy Spirit on all Ministers of the Gospel; that He would bless and prosper the means of education, and spread the light of Christian knowledge through the remotest corners of the earth.

As justification for rebelling against the King of England, and for victory on the battlefield, the colonists regularly sought the favor of Almighty God. Since England was the "Superpower" of that era, winning the Revolutionary War required the favor of Almighty God. Our forefathers knew and understood this. By seeking God's will for all that they did, once victory was achieved, they did not forget who was responsible for what had been achieved.

At the conclusion of the Revolutionary War, on November 8, 1783, John Hancock, the Governor of Massachusetts, declared:

> The Citizens of these United States have every Reason for Praise and Gratitude to the God of their salvation… I do… appoint… the 11th day of December next (the day recommended by the Congress to all the States) to be religiously observed as a Day of Thanksgiving and Prayer, that all the people may then assemble to celebrate… that he hath been pleased to continue to us the Light of the Blessed Gospel… That we also offer up fervent supplications… to cause pure Religion and Virtue to flourish… and to fill the world with his glory.

As you can see, based on quotes for these primary documents, our founding fathers not only believed in God, but they also looked to Him for wisdom, favor in battle, and leadership.

Our victory in the Revolution, which created the greatest nation in the history of the world, was made possible because Almighty

God favored our forefathers. He blessed their endeavors because they made a conscious choice to seek Him through prayer, fasting, and humiliation. (Humiliation is more accurately defined as repentance in the twenty-first century.)

The beliefs of our Revolutionary forefathers became the core convictions for the first generation of independent Americans. The God they called upon was the Christian God of the Bible—the Father of Jesus Christ—and none other.

They did not call upon Allah, nor did they submit to him. Being a false god, this wasn't even a consideration for the victors of the Revolutionary War. Instead, they embraced the Judeo-Christian Ethic as the foundation for their core convictions and governed based on this belief system, never considering any other.

To claim anything different would not only be misleading, but it would be a false statement that failed to take into account the historical record. To assert that Islam was an integral part of the foundation of America is not so, but to the politically correct Progressives, it has become undisputed truth. Additionally, in the Totalitarianism of Thought imposed on our nation, it has now become hate speech for Christians like us to assert the truth.

The generation of Revolutionaries didn't have any misgiving about who their Divine Benefactor was. They were crystal clear that it was Almighty God. This is why, John Langdon, Governor of New Hampshire, shortly after the War, on February 21, 1786, proclaimed a Day of Public Fasting and Prayer.

> It having been the laudable practice of this State, at the opening of the Spring, to set apart a day... to... penitently confess their manifold sins and transgressions, and fervently implore the divine benediction, that a true spirit of repentance and humiliation may be poured out upon all... that he would be pleased to bless the great Council of the United States of America and direct their deliberations... that he would rain down righteousness upon the earth, revive religion, and spread abroad the knowledge of the true God, the Saviour of man, throughout the world. And all servile labor and recreations are forbidden on said day.

That Christianity was essential to the formation of the United States of America is irrefutable. The same week Congress passed the Bill of Rights, President George Washington declared:

> It is the duty of all nations to acknowledge the Providence of Almighty God, to obey His will... and humbly to implore His protection and favor; and Whereas both Houses of Congress have by their joint Committee requested me "to recommend to the People of the United States a Day of Public Thanksgiving and Prayer to be observed by acknowledging with grateful hearts the many significant favors of Almighty God, especially by affording them an opportunity peaceably to establish a form of government for their safety and happiness.

I do recommend... the 26th day of November next, to be devoted by the People of these United States to the service of that great and glorious Being, who is the beneficent Author of all the good that was, that is, or that will be; That we may then all unite in rendering unto Him our sincere and humble thanks... for the peaceable and rational manner in which we have been enabled to establish constitutions of government for our safety and happiness, and particularly the national one now lately instituted, for the civil and religious liberty with which we are blessed... Humbly offering our prayers... to the great Lord and Ruler of Nations, and beseech Him to pardon our national and other transgressions.

James Madison, known as the "Chief Architect of the Constitution," wrote many of the Federalist Papers, which convinced the States to ratify the Constitution. He also introduced the First Amendment in the first session of Congress. During the War of 1812, President James Madison proclaimed a Day of Prayer, July 9, 1812, stating:

I do therefore recommend... rendering the Sovereign of the Universe... public homage... acknowledging the transgressions which might justly provoke His divine displeasure... seeking His merciful forgiveness... and with a reverence for the unerring precept of our holy religion, to do to others as they would require that others should do to them.

Calling upon Americans to seek God's will became a significant part of our core value system. On July 23, 1813, being at war with Britain once again, Madison issued a Day of Prayer:

> In the present time of public calamity and war a day may be... observed by the people of the United States as a Day of Public Humiliation and Fasting and of Prayer to Almighty God for the safety and welfare of these States... of confessing their sins and transgressions, and of strengthening their vows of repentance... that He would be graciously pleased to pardon all their offenses.

Half a century later, as the United States expanded Westward, the conflict between the slave states and the non-slave states intensified, threatening our national existence. On December 14, 1860, shortly before Lincoln took office, President James Buchanan issued a Proclamation for a National Day of Humiliation, Fasting, and Prayer.

> In this the hour of our calamity and peril to whom shall we resort for relief but to the God of our fathers? His omnipotent arm only can save us from the awful effects of our own crimes and follies... Let us... unite in humbling ourselves before the Most High, in confessing our individual and national sins... Let me invoke every individual, in whatever sphere of life he may be placed, to feel a personal responsibility to God and his country for keeping this day holy.

Nevertheless, conflict could not be averted. On August 12, 1861, after the Union lost the Battle of Bull Run, President Abraham Lincoln proclaimed:

It is fit... to acknowledge and revere the Supreme Government of God; to bow in humble submission to His chastisement; to confess and deplore their sins and transgressions in the full conviction that the fear of the Lord is the beginning of wisdom... Therefore I, Abraham Lincoln... do appoint the last Thursday in September next as a Day of Humiliation, Prayer, and Fasting for all the people of the nation.

On March 30, 1863, with the Civil War not progressing well for the Union, President Abraham Lincoln proclaimed another National Day of Humiliation, Fasting, and Prayer. It became one of his most famous statements.

The awful calamity of civil war... may be but a punishment inflicted upon us for our presumptuous sins to the needful end of our national reformation as a whole people... We have forgotten God... We have vainly imagined, in the deceitfulness of our hearts, that all these blessings were produced by some superior wisdom and virtue of our own. Intoxicated with unbroken success, we have become... too proud to pray to the God that made us! It behooves us then to humble ourselves before the offended Power, to confess our national sins.

With the assassination of President Lincoln, which shocked the world, President Johnson issued a special proclamation on April 29, 1865. It stated in part:

> The 25th day of next month was recommended as a Day for Special Humiliation and Prayer in consequence of the assassination of Abraham Lincoln... but Whereas my attention has since been called to the fact that the day aforesaid is sacred to large numbers of Christians as one of rejoicing for the ascension of the Savior: Now... I, Andrew Johnson, President of the United States, do suggest that the religious services recommended as aforesaid should be postponed until... the 1st day of June.

As stated earlier, at the end of the Great War, which began in 1914, President Wilson proclaimed on May 11, 1918, to be a day of prayer, fasting, and humiliation.

> It being the duty peculiarly incumbent in a time of war humbly and devoutly to acknowledge our dependence on Almighty God and to implore His aid and protection... I, Woodrow Wilson... proclaim... a Day of Public Humiliation, Prayer, and Fasting, and do exhort my fellow-citizens... to pray Almighty God that He may forgive our sins.

From that time until now, nearly a hundred years later, there has not been a Presidential Proclamation calling for a Day of Prayer, Fasting, and Repentance. When President Wilson called on Americans to pray, fast, and repent for God's favor in the war, they did, and there were some surprising results.

Less than a month later, the U.S. Army, led by General "Black Jack" Pershing, joined their French and British allies and fought the battle of Cantigny. It was America's first engagement in World War I.

During this battle, Medal of Honor winner Sergeant Alvin York and his men were in a desperate fight, where they were pinned down by heavy German gunfire. Many soldiers were dying. Knowing they would not survive, Sergeant York went on the offensive. He personally destroyed thirty-two German machine guns, killing twenty-eight enemy troops. In addition, he captured 132 others all by himself.

York later declared, "I'm telling you, the hand of God must have been in that fight… With all those machine guns fixed on me, and pistols besides—then those soldiers charging me with fixed bayonets—I never even received a scratch…. I've got only one explanation. God must have heard my prayers."

After the war, York's heroics were made into a movie, *Sergeant York,* starring Gary Cooper, who won an Academy Award for Best Actor. The key is that Wilson beseeched Almighty God for our entire nation, while Sergeant York's prayer was for the safety of his fellow soldiers and himself. In His benevolence, the Holy Spirit moved to not only protect our nation but also a humble soldier like Alvin York of Tennessee.

There have been other times since Woodrow Wilson's day that Presidents have called for prayer. For example, in World War II, during the D-Day invasion of Normandy, Franklin D. Roosevelt prayed publicly on the radio for the entire nation to hear. On that fateful day, June 6, 1944, Roosevelt prayed:

> Almighty God, our sons, pride of our nation, this day have set upon a mighty endeavor, a struggle to preserve our Republic, our Religion and our Civilization, and to set free a suffering humanity... Help us, Almighty God, to rededicate ourselves in renewed faith in Thee in this hour of great sacrifice.

When World War II concluded, with victory in Europe and over Japan, President Truman declared a Day of Prayer. It occurred the day after hostilities ended, on August 16, 1945. Speaking to the American people, Truman said:

> The warlords of Japan... have surrendered unconditionally... This is the end of the... schemes of dictators to enslave the peoples of the world... Our global victory... has come with the help of God... Let us... dedicate ourselves to follow in His ways.

Being true to his convictions, and knowing how unsafe the world had become in the thermonuclear era, in the last year of his Presidency in 1952, President Truman made the National Day of Prayer an annual observance. He said, "In times of national crisis, when we are striving to strengthen the foundations of peace, we stand in special need of Divine support."

More recent Presidents, including Richard Nixon, Ronald Reagan, and George W. Bush, have called for prayer but with less emphasis than leaders from earlier times in American history. Furthermore, the idea of connecting prayer, fasting, and repentance, which is clearly biblical, has come into disuse.

Perhaps, because of our perceived military invincibility, we have felt less needful of God's supernatural protection. Or is the reason for this because our more conservative Presidents do not want to make themselves vulnerable to the chastisement and relentless criticism of the Progressive Left for doing so? Maybe it's a combination of many things, but it is a mistake. There is never a right reason to do a wrong thing.

We owe our very existence as a nation to those who recognized our need for Divine intervention and guidance. For most of our history, our Presidents have understood the power that comes from the American people bowing their knees collectively to Almighty God in prayer, while fasting and repenting for our nation for our collective sins. It is the basis for our nation's strength.

Knowing this to be true, and being completely aware that we must embrace the values of our forefathers to make America great again, at *In God We Trust*, it is our intention to press the issue of prayer and call for a National Day of Prayer, Fasting, and Repentance.

Raise Up Men and Women of Character

Please Join Us in the Following Prayer

Lord God, Almighty
Where are Your mighty men—Your men of old?
Those who want to serve You with a willing heart—
Never for sordid gain, never exploiting the helplessly weak.
Why are men like these missing from our public life?
Where are the women of rectitude and honor?
Women who would rather die than dishonor Your name?
Why do we have to settle for representation that can do
Nothing more than lead by doing what is expediently popular,
Seeking wisdom from focus groups, rather than from Your will?
These evil-doers smile reassuringly, always playing a role,
But in their calculating hearts, they seek nothing more
Than personal fame and fortune—
All at the expense of the public.
Their duplicity is astounding, as they seek an advantage
Over those they have sworn to serve and to protect.

We are being led astray by men and women in the media
Who serve the false hopes of godless Progressivism.
Smiling and personable,
These narcissistic miscreants never serve.
Instead, championing false political leaders,

They deceive the righteous,
While they cheer those who rape our nation
Of its wealth, accumulated from generations past.
Never forthright,
These scoundrels bestow approbation on the unworthy.
Showing no regard for You—our benefactor
Since our founding,
They contemptuously call right wrong,
Much to the delight of misguided fools.
Because of the failed leadership in the recent past,
Our influence throughout the world has weakened appreciably,
As the false god of Islam overwhelms Europe,
While greedily eyeing America.

When will it be enough, Father?
When will You lift Your mighty hand
And stir Your people from the foolishness of their lethargy?
There are so few of us who are willing to stand and be counted.
Instead, there are a vast numbers who call on Your name
But who are unwilling to take a stand,
Choosing instead to play it safe.
Oh how we loathe the dishonor brought upon Your name.
They choose to be accommodating,
Rather than opting to be resolute,
Excusing the wickedness of Progressivism's deceitfulness—
They never stand against the false truths of the reprobates.
They willfully deceive themselves, believing that all will be well

As they sing pleasant melodies of praise to You in church.

They fool themselves, but they cannot fool You, Father.
We do not deserve to be spared
From decades of abandoning You.
We have brought about our own decline
And are without excuse.
We have willfully abandoned what is right for half a century.
Our children believe they are entitled, which makes them weak.
None are prepared for the days of darkness that lie ahead,
Nor have they forged the character necessary
To be resilient in adversity.
Without the active intervention of Your Holy Spirit,
We have no hope.
But, in Your Sovereignty, You can spare us,
If You choose to do so.
Will You, Lord?
Will You spare us for the sake of the faithful few?
We pray that You will, and we ask this
In the name of Your Son,
Amen.

CHAPTER 6

The Power of Prayer, Fasting, and Repentance

Therefore humble yourselves under the mighty hand of God,
that He may exalt you at the proper time,
casting all your anxiety upon Him,
because He cares for you.
Be of sober spirit, be on the alert.
Your adversary, the devil, prowls around
like a roaring lion, seeking someone to devour.
But resist him
(I Peter 5:6-9a, NAS).

America is important because our Kingdom mission is important. This is why patriotic Christians like us need to step up in the war for the heart and soul of America and be counted. For us, appropriating the full armor of God is our weaponry; implementing united prayer and fasting is what we use to change our nation's direction.

As Christians, we understand prayer is the primary vehicle we have been given to communicate with our Heavenly Father. Through prayer we express gratitude, reveal what is troubling our hearts, and state the deepest desires of our heart. Prayer is also the specific way we ask for our requests to be answered by God.

Prayer

Often religious leaders make prayer very difficult to understand and complicated to do. Jesus gave His disciples a model by which to pray in Matthew 6:9-13

"Pray, then, in this way:
'Our Father who is in heaven,
Hallowed be Your name.
'Your kingdom come.
Your will be done,
On earth as it is in heaven.
'Give us this day our daily bread.
'And forgive us our debts, as we also have forgiven our debtors.
'And do not lead us into temptation, but deliver us
from evil. For Yours is the kingdom and the power and the
glory forever.
Amen.'

Praying is simply talking to God. He enjoys being with His children, listening to their prayers. He also desires to talk back to us. It's a two-way conversation. Because this is so important, the Scriptures have a great deal to say about prayer. It's how we align our will with God's will:

This is the confidence which we have before Him, that, if we ask anything according to His will, He hears us (1 John 5:14, NAS).

In our prayers, we are encouraged to be confident before God, even bold, but we are not to be timid:

Therefore let us draw near with confidence to the throne of grace, so that we may receive mercy and find grace to help in time of need (Hebrews 4:16, NAS).

In God's Word, we are also encouraged to speak from our hearts. Because He loves us, our Heavenly Father wants us to tell Him exactly what we want and why. Knowing how timid we can be, the Scriptures are very clear about praying with a believing heart, as the following four biblical promises confirm:

Ask, and it will be given to you; seek, and you will find; knock, and it will be opened to you. "For everyone who asks receives, and he who seeks finds, and to him who knocks it will be opened." Or what man is there among you who, when his son asks for a loaf, will give him a stone? (Matthew 7:7-11, NAS.)

Whatever you ask in My name, that will I do, so that the Father may be glorified in the Son. "If you ask Me anything in My name, I will do it" (John 14:13-14, NAS).

Therefore I say to you, all things for which you pray and ask, believe that you have received them, and they will be granted you (Mark 11:24, NAS).

And all things you ask in prayer, believing, you will receive (Matthew 21:22, NAS).

When Christians are in agreement about what they are seeking, it is very powerful. Plus, being in one accord is exactly what our Heavenly Father desires from us. When a great multitude of believers are in agreement, like we are about America remaining free and safe from attack, it is very compelling. Our corporate prayers can be very influential before the Throne of God. Specifically, the Bible promises:

[I]f two of you agree on earth about anything that they may ask, it shall be done for them by My Father who is in heaven (Matthew 18:19a, NAS).

Our attitude while praying is crucial. Being in the proper state of mind makes all the difference in the world. Although we are told to come boldly, we are also exhorted to be humble. God resists the proud, but He gives grace to the unassuming, which is what we intend to be.

O LORD, You have heard the desire of the humble; You will strengthen their heart, You will incline Your ear (Psalm 10:17, NAS).

Recognizing our vulnerability, and representing our entire nation, we understand the looming danger of Radical Islamists and godless Progressives. This is why we are asking God to protect us and keep us free.

Call upon Me in the day of trouble; I shall rescue you, and you will honor Me (Psalm 50:15, NAS).

Recognizing that the "day of trouble" is upon us; in humility, on bended knee, it is our intention to come before the Throne of God in unity, fasting and in repentance, to ask our Heavenly Father to protect our nation, the United States of America, and to keep us safe from attack and from the false teaching of the Progressives that will lead to our destruction.

Fasting

Fasting is an important biblical principle. Although it has fallen into disuse in recent decades; in the Old Testament it was always observed on occasions of public catastrophe. Because our nation has drifted so far away from our historical purpose, to turn the ship of state around, combining prayer with fasting is very important.

Fasting supercharges our prayers, When we do both together in unity, nothing is impossible for us (Mark 9:23).

Here is my simple definition of fasting. Fasting is to temporarily set aside something that gives me natural pleasure, replacing it with spiritually focused time with God.

In the books of Daniel, I Samuel, Nehemiah and others, fasting was accompanied by prayer and confession of Israel's sins. For Daniel, fasting helped him focus on God. Daniel wrote:

So I gave my attention to the Lord God to seek Him by prayer and supplications, with fasting, sackcloth and ashes (Daniel 9:3, NAS).

Fasting was also important to the Lord. At the beginning of Christ's ministry, He went into the desert to focus on fulfilling His Father's will. In His testing time in the wilderness, fasting was part of how He began His transition into ministry.

And after He had fasted forty days and forty nights, He then became hungry (Matthew 4:2, NAS).

In the early church, times of prayer were routinely accompanied by fasting. This can be seen numerous times in the Book of Acts.

While they were ministering to the Lord and fasting, the Holy Spirit said, "Set apart for Me Barnabas and Saul for the work to which I have called them." Then, when they had fasted and prayed and laid their hands on them, they sent them away (Acts 13:2-3, NAS).

The Old Testament, as well as the New Testament, teaches the value of fasting, which is abstaining from food or drink for a certain period, in order to focus on seeking God's will through prayer and supplication. Based on the examples of those who fasted in the Bible, we know that God grants supernatural revelation and wisdom through this practice. This biblical principle is clear and indisputable.

Additionally, Scripture teaches us that fasting will help us grow and achieve a more intimate relationship with our Heavenly Father. It is for this reason, and because our purpose is so significant, that it will be a consistent part of our outreach.

Repentance

The Scriptural mandate for our entire outreach is found in 2 Chronicles 7:14. Originally spoken by God concerning Israel's rebellious nature, its value has not diminished, nor has it changed. We are still called upon to humble ourselves before Almighty God and turn from our wicked ways, which is exactly what repentance is.

If my people, which are called by my name, shall humble themselves, and pray, and seek my face, and turn from their wicked ways; then will I hear from heaven, and will forgive their sin, and will heal their land (2 Chronicles 7:14, NAS).

As our nation continues to drift further away from God and the values of our founding fathers, our nation has become willful and arrogant. In our reprobate thinking, which is what Progressivism really is, we have called right wrong and wrong right.

Even worse, we have legislated Evil to be the law of the land in many areas of our life. This behavior, institutionalizing Evil, is specifically what we are publicly confessing as sin. Consistently, without sugarcoating the truth, we intend to openly acknowledge what is wrong in America. It's the only way to accomplish our goal.

Preach the word; be ready in season and out of season; reprove, rebuke, exhort, with great patience and instruction (II Timothy 4:2, NAS).

The wrongdoing of our nation has been so shocking that our transgressions have gone over our head. Individually, our power to confront societal Evil may be limited, but corporately we have incredible strength, not just in a political sense, but also as God's children before His Throne.

Therefore, on numerous occasions throughout the year, we intend to pray, fast, and repent of our societal issues. We are doing this, not only individually, but also as the corporate Body of Christ. This makes our effort, which includes what you do, very important. The areas of repentance will include at least the following, but there are other areas as well:

1. Since the Supreme Court decision on *Roe v. Wade* in 1973, there have been more than 58 million babies aborted legally, including many partial-birth abortions. This is the equivalent of every man, woman, and child living in Texas, New York, and Michigan.

2. As a nation, we have been prideful and arrogant, turning our backs on God, as if we became the most powerful nation in the history of the world by ourselves, rather than as a result of His benevolence, mercy, grace, and favor.

3. Worshiping celebrities as people to emulate, we have valued fame, youth, and notoriety above estimable character qualities like love, joy, peace, patience, and kindness. The end result of our distorted perspective is this: we have permitted the entertainment industry to pollute our cul-

ture and the mind's of our youth with anti-American and anti-Christian values.

4. We repeatedly elect leaders who do not stand for our traditional Judeo-Christian biblical value system. Instead, we have bestowed power on men and women who have virtually no moral compass—people who champion the cause of depraved immorality.

5. Even in our churches, truth has become relative. We are being led by many pastors who compromise the inerrancy of the Bible. They have become more interested in being popular than in being righteous.

6. Denying God's precepts, we have become a nation where everybody does what is right in his or her own eyes. Of specific importance, and to our discredit, we do not stand up and defend the biblical definition of marriage.

7. Mocking God and the wisdom of the Bible, we have allowed our colleges and universities to teach Progressivism to our young men and women. As a consequence, higher education has become the spawning ground for anti-American and anti-Christian thought.

8. We have become a "Stoner Nation," but not just from illegal drugs. We have also permitted "Big Pharma" to flood our nation with addictive pain medication, producing an opioid and heroin epidemic. More people die from drug overdoses than from cancer.

9. Being passive, we have accepted social segregation and racism without making a stand for justice. There is no justification or wiggle room for racism, especially for Christians. If Christ died for the sins of all, and He did, then we are all equal in the eyes of God.

10. As believers, especially baby boomers, we have focused on our personal lives like we have tunnel vision. We do not love our neighbors like we love ourselves. Having such a mindset is sinful and detrimental to God's Kingdom. Pursuing abundance and acquiring material things over service, we have abandoned our first love.

11. In our repudiation of God's will, precepts, and leadership, we have embraced a spirit of lawlessness that empowers the shameful at the expense of our most vulnerable citizens. As organized agitators riot in the streets of major cities and universities across the land, creating havoc and destruction—as they try to impose their will on those who desire peace and tranquility—they are championed by the Progressives. They not only destroy property, but also tear at the fabric of our society.

This list is not complete, nor was it intended to be so. Feel free to add to it. It does, however, show the enormity of the problem we are facing. Clearly, national repentance is in order, and it must begin with the people who have been chosen to be salt to the world and light to our society. This means it begins with us—not just some of us, all of us.

As a place to begin, here is a prayer for you. It will help prepare your heart and your mind for the task that lies ahead of us. It's a call to action, not just for us, but also for Almighty God.

Pray it as often as you desire. There is no downside to repeating it frequently, even daily. Add to it or subtract from it, as you feel led. Do whatever feels the most comfortable to you. Here it is:

Almighty God, Save Our Nation

Please Join Us in the Following Prayer

Father, Lord God, Almighty
We come to You today, in humility, kneeling before you,
As penitents in need of Your intervention for America.
Throughout our history, even in our darkest days,
During the Revolution, Civil War, World Wars,
And the Great Depression,
When our survival was threatened,
You have always been there for us.
In each of our times of calamity and distress,
You have been faithful,
Leading and guiding us to safety,
But we need You now more than ever.
We have been proud and arrogant,
Condescending and greedy,
As we willingly chose to walk in the ways of darkness.

Disregarding Your precepts,
We have called right wrong and wrong right.
America is no longer what it once was,
Nor even a close proximity.
With depravity escalating daily,
While righteousness diminishes,
Our nation has foolishly followed a path
That will lead to our destruction.

Because we, Your children, fear for America's future, we come
Before You on bended knee, to seek
Your forgiveness for America.
In Your graciousness, Father, restore us to what we once were—
To the people who risked life and limb, simply to worship You
In purity and in peace. We admit the way America is traveling
Does not honor You, Your Name, or
Your purpose for our future.
In our relentless pursuit of self-indulgence,
Greed and pleasure,
We have pursued selfish goals,
While disregarding the needs of others,
Especially the unborn,
Who remain perpetually voiceless in our society.

Father, we know Your Word says,
"Woe to those who call evil good,"
But this is exactly what our nation has done.
Institutionalizing depravity,

We have called it normal,
While caustically rebuking the righteous.
In our culture's hostility to Your truth,
We have vigorously imposed
Totalitarianism of thought on those who disagree with
The politically correct pontifications of our haughty leaders.
Left to indulge in the pursuit of perverted self-gratification,
Which is being championed
By the distortions of Progressivism,
Our nation may never again stand up for Your mandates.
Instead, with cavalier bravado, we have become like a lemming,
Racing headlong toward the cliff
Of our societal self-destruction.

In this dangerous world, we are unsafe at home and abroad.
Radical Islamic Jihadism relentlessly seeks to destroy our land
And subjugate our people, forcing us to worship their false god,
Knowing You, we will never submit,
But there are those among us
Who dismiss this threat with a careless attitude
Of false confidence.
In the foolishness of their folly, they scoff at those of us
Who recognize Radical Islam for what it really is,
Including its goals.
Because we are Your children,
We understand this perpetual threat.
Father, having wandered far from You,
America has abandoned

Our national slogan, "In God We Trust."
We no longer honor You.
We are without excuse.
The gravity of our sin is ever before us,
But You are slow to anger and full of
Love, grace, and mercy.
Be gracious to us.
We ask this, not based on any righteousness
Of our own, but on Your compassionate, forgiving nature.

On behalf of our nation,
The United States of America, we come
Before You today, with knees bent,
Asking that You keep us safe
From foreign enemies and wicked terrorists who want to
Destroy and enslave us.
Also, protect the naive from the poison
Of Progressivism and its depraved
Mindset that is so destructive.
We acknowledge that our nation has been willfully disobedient,
And we are undeserving of Your favor,
But because we are Your children,
Who have been redeemed by
The Blood of Your Son, Jesus Christ,
We come before You boldly today and ask these things of You,
In the Name of Jesus Christ,
Amen.

CONCLUSION

Therefore humble yourselves under the mighty hand of God,
that He may exalt you at the proper time
(I Peter 5:6, NAS).

How many times in your life have you said or heard another person say, "They need to do something about that?" It has probably happened quite often, hasn't it? The "somebody," of course, is rarely identified, and nothing ever seems to get done about the problem that needs to be solved.

In many ways, this typifies the way we have dealt with the issues we are facing in America, none of which ever seem to get resolved—not in the way most of us believe they should be handled anyway. The responsibility for changing undesired situations always seems to belong to someone else—to some nameless, faceless, entity. In our minds, it's never our responsibility, and it doesn't belong to us.

Consequently, we remain perpetually frustrated. We routinely feel powerless to rectify each of the situations that trouble us, regardless of how serious they become. It's as if we have no power at all, and frustration is our only legitimate recourse. We have become like the proverbial frog in a pot of warm water that doesn't realize how hot it is becoming until the water is boiling and it is too late.

Without any desire to have done so, patriotic Christians in America have acted like frogs. We have watched in horror, as the moral character of our nation has atrophied to the point where the United States no longer seems like the nation it once was. We have witnessed wrong being legalized and what is correct being criminalized, and all we have done about it is shake our heads in disgust and bewilderment.

But it doesn't need to be this way. We are not powerless; we are far from it. We can be the people who "do something" about the issues that trouble us, and there are many of them. Individually, there may not be much we can do, but corporately, as members of the Body of Christ, we have power beyond our wildest imaginations.

When we come together and unite, humbling ourselves before Almighty God in prayer, accompanied by fasting and repentance, our power and authority are expanded and enhanced exponentially. When we exercise our power through united prayer, not only will the world shake but the heavens will tremble. This is the kind of authority the Body of Christ has. When it is done for His glory, this is the way believers can harness His power and authority.

By joining together to come before Almighty God on behalf of the United States corporately, as the Body of Christ, we can petition the Holy Spirit of God to create national revival, and this is exactly what we intend to do. We want to change the course of our nation and the course of history.

As individuals, this would just be a dream but, when it is our corporate goal, with our united voices beseeching the Throne of God, we can make a difference that will change the world. Together, with so many participating, including you, our vision can become a reality.

We still believe America is a "City on a Hill" for the world to emulate. Having wandered from our original vision, we need to get back on the right track again.

Although we are all Americans, the fundamental gap between the beliefs of the Progressives and patriotic believing Americans is as wide as the Grand Canyon. Because we have not been paying attention, the Progressives have gained a solid foothold in several key areas of American life. Although most of them have been voted out of office, they have a firm hold on the media, our colleges, and high schools. Our young people are being indoctrinated into a belief system that is godless and anti-American.

To be faithful to our convictions and to the Lord, we must make a firm commitment to oppose Progressivism at every turn. It is a domestic enemy to our Constitution and to our American way of life. Through political correctness, they have taken away our voice for long enough, but we must no longer be willing to allow this.

It's time for us to stand up and take our nation back. It's time for us to be the light and salt to the world that Almighty God has destined us to be. It's time for us to be faithful. If not now, when? If not us, who?

It's time for us to stand together. Will you be one of these people? Will you stand with us? Will you make the commitment to be part of *In God We Trust*? And will you keep this commitment? America is worth the effort. In your heart, you know it is.

When we join together in the power of the Holy Spirit, we can not only make America safe again, but we can also fulfill God's call on us individually and as a nation. It is with this mission in mind that we proudly stand together and proudly proclaim (just as our founders did) that it is—In God We Trust!

Preach the word; be ready in season and out of season; reprove,
rebuke, exhort, with great patience and instruction
(II Timothy 4:2, NAS).

APPENDIX

Prayers for America's Safety

Prayer for When Flight 11 Hit North Trade Center

Our Heavenly Father,
We remember where we were that day,
The day when the hijacked plane hit the North Tower
Of the World Trade Center in New York City.
It's a memory that has been forever etched on our minds.
It was an assault that scarred the soul of our great nation,
Creating anxiety, fear, and trepidation among our citizens.
Like the attack on Pearl Harbor that started World War II,
The sneak attack on 9/11 has become another day of infamy.
Stunned by the destruction of the Twin Towers, we have come
To understand the severity of what happened in 2001.
Over time, our vulnerability has become abundantly clear.

It was at that precise moment every American realized
We were no longer safe because of the
Vast oceans surrounding us.
We have become susceptible to an enemy who wants
To destroy the land of the free and the home of the brave.
Because of the magnitude of the vast carnage
We suffered that day, and the fervent hatred for America
By those who precipitated the strike,

Our world was changed, and it will never be the same again.
Acknowledging this, we come before You today in humility,
Fasting to harness our minds and our bodies for our great need.
Father, we are a penitent people,
Desirous of Your benevolent mercy.
As believing Christians,
We come before You on behalf of the nation
We love so much, seeking Your mercy and Your favor.

There are still multiplied millions who wish us ill—those who
Want to destroy this great nation and our Christian heritage.
They intend to subjugate Your children to a false god,
Which is not what we desire, nor is it Your will.
Father, we need You to protect us from this damnable fate.
In Your benevolence, have compassion on us and guard us.
We know and acknowledge that
We do not deserve Your blessing.
Our generation has abandoned Your way
And been cavalier about it.
In our willful arrogance, we have discarded Your leadership,
Choosing to embrace the godlessness of Progressivism,
Instead of the righteous paths established by our forefathers,
The road we are now traveling has not been ordained by You.
It will only lead to further ruin,
heartache, and disillusionment.
Nothing good will come from it,
which we know and lament.

This is why we cry out to You today—
At the exact moment
When our vulnerability became evident
For the world to see.
Protect us, Father.
Let us enjoy peace and prosperity once again,
Safe from the attacks of enemies
Who continuously plot against us.
Let us look to the future with confident, righteous assurance,
Knowing that our God is greater than their false god.
Father, we gladly bow our knees to You,
As Your obedient children.
You are the Architect of our destiny
And can foil their Evil plans.

Bring to ruin and calamity those who loathe You and hate
Your children—
Those of us who willingly bear Your name.
Do not allow the Evil of our enemies to triumph over America.
Refresh us, Father. Permit righteousness to once again prevail,
As we soberly reflect in prayer, with fasting and repentance,
On this day, the day we were attacked sixteen years ago.
It is our corporate prayer for You
To stir the American people
To turn from their wicked ways, repent, and embrace Your will.
We ask this in the Name of Your precious Son, Jesus Christ,
Amen.

Prayer for When Flight 175 Hit South Trade Center

Father, Lord God, Almighty,
We remember, we remember well,
When the second hijacked plane hit the South Tower.
This is when it became crystal clear that
This was not an accident.
This was not some bizarre miscalculation by a pilot.
We were under attack. Some unknown force,
Wanting to destroy the United States of America
Has knowingly and willfully set a plan in motion
To crush the American spirit and to bring us to our knees,
But those evil Islamic Terrorists do not know us.
They do not understand the American people,
Nor do they know our God.

Father, those Jihadists who attacked us on 9/11 are all dead,
But their hatred for the United States remains strong,
As a new generation of Radical Islamic Terrorists
Target the land of the free and the home of the brave.
We are far wiser now, having bolstered our defenses,
But we are not impervious to attack—far from it.
We need You to keep us safe. We need You to foil
The plots of those who wish to destroy us.
We know this, and we know the fear it has created
In the hearts of Americans—an apprehensiveness
That only Your peace can counteract.

This is why we are coming to you today,
At the exact time the second Tower was hit,
In fasting and prayer, confessing the sins of our nation,
Which are so egregious they go over our head.
Father, protect us and keep us safe, not because
We are deserving and have followed Your leading,
But because You are merciful, slow to anger,
And have always been there for America in time of need.
We ask this in the name of Your Son, Jesus Christ,
Amen.

CPSIA information can be obtained
at www.ICGtesting.com
Printed in the USA
BVOW06s0434130717
489179BV00007B/15/P